# Cornfields
## to
# Codfish

# Cornfields
## to
# Codfish

### Musings

*To Barb,*
*In celebration*
*of the places*
*we call home!*

Linda Malcolm

*Linda Malcolm*

**iUniverse**

# CORNFIELDS TO CODFISH MUSINGS

*iUniverse books may be ordered through booksellers or by contacting:*

*iUniverse*
*1663 Liberty Drive*
*Bloomington, IN 47403*
*www.iuniverse.com*
*1-800-Authors (1-800-288-4677)*

*Cornfields to Codfish* may also be ordered through the author's website: www.lindamalcolm.com.

*Because of the dynamic nature of the Internet, any web addresses or links contained in this book may have changed since publication and may no longer be valid. The views expressed in this work are solely those of the author and do not necessarily reflect the views of the publisher, and the publisher hereby disclaims any responsibility for them.*

*ISBN: 978-1-5320-8511-6 (sc)*
*ISBN: 978-1-5320-8512-3 (e)*

*Library of Congress Control Number: 2019915893*

*Print information available on the last page.*

*iUniverse rev. date: 11/05/2019*

# Contents

## Cornfields

## Interlude

## Codfish

# A Menagerie of Recipes

# Preface

Twenty-five years after moving away from the farm in Iowa, I realized that my people, my family, and our way of life are just as rich and complex as those sprinkled across the globe.

I am a culture junkie, a person with affection and admiration for foreign cultures and unfamiliar places. This fascination began to bloom in 1984, my freshman year at Luther College. The campus of this small liberal arts school is set within walking distance of Decorah, the most Norwegian town in Iowa. At Luther, I was surrounded by a student population largely of Scandinavian descent. Fascinated, I wholeheartedly slipped into and ate up this beautiful culture that was foreign to me.

When home for Christmas my freshman year, I added a Norwegian food tradition to my family's celebration: lefse. Following the recipe of a college friend's grandmother, I boiled potatoes, not for dinner but rather to mash with flour, sugar, a little salt, and a splash of cream. Then, pulling enough dough off to flatten into a disk resembling a large flour tortilla, I dry-fried both sides in a hot cast iron skillet. When the dough had a few brown spots on either side, I flipped it onto a plate, spread butter over it, sprinkled it with cinnamon and sugar, and folded it in half and then half again to create a sweet layered lefse treat. This Norwegian culinary phenomenon became a holiday tradition with my family for several years. Until I introduced them to Irish Potato Chowder.

In the mid-80s, I joined in with the Norwegians as they joked about lutefisk, although I had never seen, smelled, or touched this gelatinous "delicacy" – also a food tradition connected to Christmas. Lutefisk starts as dried whitefish, usually cod. Prior to eating, it is soaked in a lye solution for a couple of days to rehydrate the fish – at this stage it is inedible. Stories and stories surround how this bizarre process started. Some point to the fish reverting to its original form with the lye soaking. To make it edible, the fish is then soaked in water for four to six days, with a daily changing of the water. Finally, it is boiled to its gelatinous state and served with butter, salt, and pepper.

In my senior year at Luther, I took out a $2,500 loan from my hometown bank to pay for a class to study architecture in London, Paris, and Amsterdam during January 1988. For "J-term," Luther students could take an in-depth course on campus for one class credit, take a month off school, or travel abroad on a faculty-led course. In the briefing before the month-long trip, our professor had a warning for us young, first-time travelers: Once you go on this trip, you will always want to travel. Forever.

That was an accurate prediction. My infatuation with travel was intense. I drank the potion. Given a plane ticket, I wouldn't ask the destination; I would go anywhere. And throughout my frequent travels in the next couple of decades, I naively wished I had my own rich, vibrant culture.

In 1992, I married Bill, an English immigrant who had the same outlook as I did. We wanted to go, to see, and to do. In our first twelve years of marriage, while we lived in Rockford, Illinois, we visited Bill's family in England, mine in Iowa, and vacationed in Germany and Paris. With another couple, we captained and crewed our own sailboat and scuba dove on week-long sails in the British and US Virgin Islands. We flew to Athens, then transferred to the coast to sail the Ionian Sea for two weeks. We ventured to Little Cayman to dive three and four times a day, reaching depths of a hundred feet. We lived on a dive boat with several friends for a week off the coast of Belize. Touching land only once in seven days, we were enthralled by the spectacular variety of fish. When the dive boat docked in Belize City, we rented a van with our friends and drove to a Mayan temple near the Belize and Guatemala border.

Over the years, we soaked up history and ate our way through these countries and islands. We exchanged smiles and used hand gestures where spoken language was a barrier. We joked that we had lived our retirement in our twenties and thirties, and we vowed that when we had children, we would keep up the same energy for travel but perhaps focus more on US travel when our kids were young.

Following a couple years of infertility, Bill and I decided that while we wanted children, we didn't need our children to be carbon copies of us. Over the course of two years, we created our family of four through adoption. Our sons, Will and Liam, were both born in South Korea.

When the boys were very young, we made trips to Iowa and to England a priority so that our sons would know their grandparents, aunts, uncles, and cousins. Throughout early elementary school, we visited our extended family and network of friends in the Midwest six to eight times a year and made annual trips to England. And we made good use of long weekends exploring New England. In the six hours that it took to drive across Iowa, we could cover a generous circle through Massachusetts, New Hampshire, Maine, and Vermont. Or even cross the Canadian border.

Then, at age 43, I was diagnosed with breast cancer. After the diagnosis in June 2009, I went through a year of surgeries, radiation, and chemotherapy. During that time, I made a choice not to travel – fearing germs because my immune system was weak. I wouldn't fly to Iowa during treatment. Not for Thanksgiving or for Christmas. Not for Easter. Not until June 2010.

During those twelve months away from Iowa, I realized that neither lefse nor lutefisk would ever be at the core of who I was. Rather, the stoic, stubborn, practical nature of being an Iowan gave me the leverage to "do" that year. Through distance created by breast cancer, I realized that the strange numbing calm that falls over me in stressful situations is a product of my Midwest heritage. As my hair grew back in the spring of 2010, I reflected on my culture as an Iowan, a Midwest farm girl, and began to write about it. I counted down the weeks until June 2010 when I would again have Mom's braised roast beef and potato dinner.

So the following pages are not filled with travel essays, nor is this book organized as a chronology of my life – moving from a farm girl in Iowa, through my twenties working as a cost accountant and my early married years in Illinois, to being a writer and a mother in Massachusetts. It's not a blow-by-blow walk through my year of surgeries, chemo, and radiation to fight breast cancer.

Instead, it's a celebration of where I grew up in the Midwest and a piecemeal exploration of our new home in New England, discovered via an indirect journey. Think of flying from Boston to Chicago but having to connect through Dallas, Minneapolis, London, Santa Fe, and Billings – the kind of journey where you may not know exactly where you are while en route, but you feel delightfully fortunate once you've arrived.

# Cornfields

---

"One place understood helps us
understand all places better."

Eudora Welty

# Meat and Potatoes

————◆◆————

Born in 1966, I was raised on a dairy farm in northeast Iowa surrounded by cornfields. I come from a meat and potatoes family. Sunday dinners featured fall-apart braised roast beef and mashed potatoes. Like my mom's dad, Granddad Bauer, and my dad's dad, Grandpa Mills, I ate my boiled, fork-mashed potatoes yellow with butter and heavily dotted with pepper. The potatoes' simple-carb cousin, sliced and buttered white bread – either store-bought or homemade by an Amish neighbor – also accompanied every meal. Mom's home-canned green beans, frozen corn, and baked squash rounded out those dinners.

It was a Sunday morning in the fall of 1986, my junior year of college, when I first realized that I come from a meat and potatoes *state*. I was driving home from Luther College, a small liberal arts school in the high northeast corner of Iowa. My mom had arranged for a family photo to be taken that afternoon, so I was making a quick hour-and-a-half trip home. Barely fifteen minutes into the drive, my 1968 olive-green Ford LTD broke down in the hills south of Decorah, Iowa.

Yes, hills in Iowa. The northeast corner of Iowa is in the "Driftless Area" of the Midwest, an area covering roughly 24,000 square miles where Iowa, Wisconsin, and Minnesota meet. This hilly land and the cliffs bordering the Mississippi River were left untouched by melting and receding glaciers that created the characteristically flat land in the middle of the country. *Drift* refers to the rubble of sand, clay, gravel, and boulders that glaciers left behind as they moved and melted over the neighboring Midwestern flatlands. Hence, the creative name of this geographic region, the Drift*less* Area.

Through the rearview mirror, I could see steam rolling out the back of the car. I was not surprised or panicked. I had paid only $200 for my green army tank, and I was on a familiar, busy highway. Immediately, a young farmer pulled up behind me. He had seen the steam and shared in my thankfulness that it hadn't been smoke. He knew a mechanic who might be willing to come out on a Sunday to tow the car in and fix it. The mechanic came and loaded up my car on his tow truck. The farmer offered to take me to his house, where I could wait with his wife while my car was being repaired. I hopped into the passenger side of his pickup truck.

A whiff of their Sunday dinner hit me when the young farmer opened the back door of their house. Dinner was ready, and pleasant words to the effect of "you might as well eat with us" were spoken in the Iowa farmer way. Grace was followed by fall-apart braised roast beef and mashed potatoes. I thought how interesting – and comforting – it was that this couple had the same Sunday dinner as my family!

Two hours later, the farmer gave me a ride to the mechanic's shop, and I was back on the road. I don't remember what the farmer or his wife looked like or where they lived. I don't remember what was wrong with my car. But that roast beef dinner – and the kindness in the invitation for me to join them – has stayed with me for decades.

# Dancing with a Foreign City Slicker

A few months before Bill and I got married in October 1992, I signed us up for ballroom dancing lessons with the intention of having our first dance as a married couple choreographed. I learned a tough lesson: in ballroom dancing, there can be only one leader – and that is normally the male's role. In our three years of dating, we had rarely argued; however, dancing revealed a power struggle previously undetected in our relationship. We both like to lead. We are both stubborn.

Bill and I met in 1989 in Rockford, Illinois, through one of my college friends. I graduated in May 1988 from Luther College, and since I didn't have a job when I graduated, I accepted my friend Ellen's invitation to share a house with her for six months in Rockford and to look for a job there. Ellen had graduated from Luther a year before me. I figured this would probably be a short stop and that I would most likely move on to another city if I hadn't found the right job within six months.

Bill coached Ellen's women's soccer team. Six weeks after Ellen first introduced us, Bill and I were on our first date, going to a Chicago Bulls game to see Michael Jordan and former University of Iowa Hawkeye B. J. Armstrong on the basketball court at the United Center in Chicago. On the way to the game, we got lost. We sensed that we were close to the stadium, but we were driving in circles without finding it. Finally, Bill pulled up next to a parked police car so I could ask for directions. The cop rolled his eyes, told us to roll up the windows and lock the doors, and then led us to the stadium. I must add that when Bill picked me up for the game, I had offered to bring a map with me. Bill assured me that there was no need for that. We arrived at halftime – but the game went into double overtime, and the Bulls won. We saw a whole game despite driving around lost for the first half.

A couple months after the Bulls game, Bill and I made the three-and-a-half-hour drive from Rockford to northeast Iowa to spend Easter with my family. After we crossed the Mississippi River and entered Iowa farm country, I began my tutorial in Manure 101.

My nose easily identified the smells along the way. I tried to describe the scents to help Bill distinguish between cow and pig. They were so distinct that I was having a hard time understanding why he couldn't pick up on the difference. Pig manure is stringent. It really stinks and lingers unpleasantly. As a friend of mine put it, pig shit gets into the pores of your skin. Cow manure is mellower; it lacks the pungency of that of the smaller-hoofed animal. Cow manure smells like home.

While this lesson entertained us for an hour and a half, I was unsuccessful as an instructor. A few years later, I realized that Bill can't smell much of anything. During that Easter road trip, he made guesses during our manure lesson just to appease me. Wooing me across my heartland.

As we unloaded luggage at my parents' house, Bill picked up his duffel bag, and I heard a clanking. I asked what it was.

"I brought a couple bottles of wine for your parents."

"Oh. . . . They don't drink."

This grandson of a London publican looked at me, bewildered.

When Bill's granddad retired from managing the Elephant & Castle Pub, he left the South Bank area of London and moved to Stevenage, where his family lived, just thirty miles north of London. Bill's granddad would pop by in the afternoon and coax Bill away from his homework and out for a beer. Bill was fourteen.

In comparison, I had my first beer – with Bill – when I was twenty-six. Bill and I were in Berghoff's, a German restaurant in Chicago. The first cold brew I consumed accompanied a plate of sausage and schnitzel. Bill's had been consumed bellying up to a bar with his granddad while under the legal drinking age of eighteen.

After Easter dinner, Bill stood up to help Mom clear the table, and amidst blank looks from all the other men still seated, he asked, "Could we save the turkey drippings for breakfast?" Mom had made gravy with turkey fat, and Bill had noticed some leftover fat in the roaster.

"Of course," my mom obligingly replied. She didn't ask questions.

The next morning, baffled by how Bill was planning to dine on drippings, Mom offered to heat them up.

"Oh, no thank you," Bill replied cheerfully. "I just spread it on toast."

"Oh . . . OK."

No one joined him.

(Sidebar: According to Bill, this year's drippings were excellent. The butter and whole herbs must have added to the flavor. I was also informed that his Black Friday tradition isn't as enjoyable if I'm in the kitchen. In my presence, he feels guilty slathering on the turkey fat. My look has nothing to do with his arteries. I'm still grossed out by the breakfast, even after more than twenty years of the tradition. I replied that he didn't have turkey drippings every day, so I really didn't mind if he had it on special occasions – as long as he didn't expect me to join in.)

Bill and I were married three years after that Easter visit, and trips to Iowa continue to be educational for all involved. Bill loves getting his hands dirty in projects with Dad and my two brothers. During one visit, Dad told Bill to get a pitchfork from the barn. Bill went to the middle of the barnyard, stopped on the gravel drive, looked at the four buildings, and then came to find me.

"Linda, there are four barns out there," he said in a frustrated tone. "How am I supposed to know which one the pitchfork is in?"

I went outside with him and started my Barnyard Building 101 tutorial. I pointed to each one and identified them: the shop, the corn crib, the hay shed, and, finally, the barn. I half expected to see Dad laughing behind one of the buildings.

A couple of years later, on another adventure in Iowa during corn-picking season, tractors, combines, and wagons were parked in the barnyard. Bill came over to me and said, "You've got to see this little field mouse by the combine tire. It's tiny and the tire is so huge." His sweet smile was filled with awe.

"It's just sitting there?" I asked, thinking it was probably sick – and how funny it was to hear it called a "field mouse." A mouse is a mouse is a mouse, no matter where it lives. And mice are rodents.

Bill nodded with a smile. I went and had a look. Dad came over to see what we were gawking at.

He looked down. "What the hell?" Then . . . stomp.

My delicate dance with a foot on either side of the Mississippi River ended with the stomp of Dad's boot. City, meet farm, a collision of unspeakable magnitude.

Dad didn't miss a beat. He went back to work. No doubt Bill's heart did miss a beat – or two. We didn't talk about the incident on Mills soil, but later that day, about the time we were driving across the Mississippi on the way home to Illinois, Bill simply said, "You know, I've been thinking about that mouse."

I tried to explain that to Dad it was a small version of a rat. That on occasion mice run up the inside of pant legs. Again, my attempt at explaining a farm phenomenon was unsuccessful.

A few months after the mouse incident, Mom and Dad were having a hog butchered, and we were taking half of the meat. Bill placed a special order when Mom wondered what cuts we wanted; he asked Mom to get the kidneys for him.

"Of course," Mom agreed. This time he explained that steak and kidney pie was a traditional food in England. I'm not sure how Mom told the butcher she wanted pork kidneys, normally considered refuse.

Our wedding dance marked the end of our dancing days. Even though we do not fox-trot on a dance floor, we have found a way to waltz through over twenty-five years of marriage. Negotiating for the lead. A bit of stepping on toes. And melding the familiarities of our two homelands into a culture of our own.

# Walking Beans

On a hot afternoon in August 2012, my sons and I flew to Iowa for our annual summer visit. We were nearing the end of the hour-plus drive from the Cedar Rapids airport to the farm when I saw Dad's truck parked near one of his bean fields. Together with my sister-in-law and nephew, Dad was walking beans: pulling weeds and cutting down volunteer corn. We had just rolled into real farming in progress.

In the 1980s, summer in Iowa brought two seasonal agricultural jobs to high school students: detasseling corn and walking beans. Today, crews of detasselers are still hired by farmers who have contracts with seed corn dealers to grow their seed corn. To produce the best seed corn, dealers direct the planting of two different strains of corn, one male and one female, in the same field. Then, before the tassels open, a crew of detasselers pulls the tassels from rows of female corn, allowing for cross-pollination when the male corn later tassels out. The wind shakes loose pollen and blows it to the tassel-free corn. Similar to vegetable and flower seeds, corn kernels from these fields are dried, stored, and sold to farmers in fifty-pound bags the following year. In 2018, my family paid $300 a bag for seed corn. One bag is enough to plant about two and a quarter acres of corn.

Friends of mine who detasseled worked through the angry heat and humidity of the afternoon. I was never a fan of that Midwestern afternoon high sun and the accompanying thick air, so I walked beans in the morning with a small, more sensible crew of eight high school friends. Unlike detasseling, the job of walking beans is now obsolete in Iowa as herbicides are applied to the soybean fields to kill volunteer corn and weeds. While that job may no longer exist, my memory of it remains strong.

Iowa farmers do not plant crops in the same location year after year. Crop rotation allows the ground to recover nutrients stripped by a crop. Dad alternates fields between hay, soybeans, and field corn. The moneymakers for the farm are soybeans and field corn, so Dad grows those on 80% of his land.

When a field of corn is harvested in October, kernels fall into the dirt as the ears of corn are shuffled between the combine hopper and the wagons moving corn from the fields to storage bins. If beans are planted in that field the following year, volunteer corn pops up in the rows. And if left to grow, the harvested soybeans will contain corn kernels. This tainting by corn lowers the market value of the beans. Consequently, when I was in high school, farmers hired crews of teenagers to walk bean fields and, using machetes or corn knives, to hack out the volunteer corn and any stray weeds.

Walking beans was my first paid job. I remember getting up before dawn, pulling on heavy, mud-laden sneakers, and packing my machete and my thermos of water in Mom and Dad's 1975 Oldsmobile. Then I drove forty minutes to meet my crew at sunrise in a bean field in the middle of a wide, flat horizon. We would mark out four rows for each walker and start off. When we came to a weed or cornstalk, we would cut its stem as low as possible and toss it between the bean rows.

I can't put a number on how long those fields were, but I know they were more than a couple hundred yards. In high school, I marched in the band, and I remember how easy it was to move from one end zone to the other. From the bean rows where we started, I squinted, looking for the end of the rows. Most mornings that destination felt like a fictional place. It was far in the distance and veiled by the morning moisture that hung over the beans. It felt like there was no end to the rows until we were only a true hundred-yard football field away.

The temperature during the days could be 95 degrees and humid, but at night the temperature dropped a bit and the air became moist, covering the bean leaves with morning dew. The edges of the leaves had a sharp feeling to them with the weight of the water. We got used to the leaves as they caught our legs with a force just short of a paper cut. Early in the morning, water soaked my shorts, calves, ankles, socks, and shoes. By 11 a.m., I would be dried out a bit, except for my soaked feet. By 12:30 p.m., we were done for the day. We bowed out when the midday sun's rays were at their strongest. I would pull my shoes and socks off before driving home so they would dry out and my pink raisin toes would regain their natural shape.

My sons' idea of farm life is vastly different from the reality I knew growing up. While the crops are the same, the farm has changed over the years from dairy cows to beef cattle, with no other livestock. No more butchering chickens with my cousins. No more collecting eggs. No more pigs. No more twice-daily milkings. No more warm cow barns. No calves sucking on fingers. My definition of farm life is very different from what my sons now experience when we go home to Iowa.

When my older son, Will, was nine years old, he showed me his digital cows in a computer game. "Watch this, Mom!" He collected a bucket, walked up to a cow, bumped her on the hip, and his bucket filled with milk.

Shocked at this gross inaccuracy, I said, "You know it doesn't really happen that way, right?"

I was answered with an eyeball roll. Will knows where the udders are, but he doesn't know the logistics of moving milk from a cow to a bucket to the table. He hasn't had the full-on multisensory smack of being in a milk barn, particularly on a winter evening:

The puff of corn dust from dumping a gallon of ground corn into the manger for the cows to eat while being milked. The two fistfuls of protein pellets sprinkling down on top of the corn. The opening of the barnyard door and the sauntering of each cow to her own stanchion. The sliding and snapping of the iron stanchion as it's locked in snugly, not tightly, to hold the cow in place while milking. The looping of the belt over the cow's back and fastening it underneath so the milk machine will have an anchor. The maneuvering of milk machines into place and attaching suctioned cups to each teat. The shift from quiet preparation to loud pumping of the engine that creates a strong suction to move milk from the cow's udder to the tub hanging on the belt. The soft figure-eights of the farm cats around ankles as they wait for dinner from the first milk machine to come off a cow. The sweetness of raw milk pouring into a strainer on top of a milk can. The rise of steam off warm milk as it hits the cold air. The building warmth of the barn as twenty cows are milked. The pour of warm, strained milk into a pitcher to take to the house. The quiet of the barn when the milk machines shut down and the cows lolling out of the barn as gently as they had come in.

This piece of my Iowan culture, milking cows, is nearly impossible to convey to my sons or my husband. However, I grinned in thankful disbelief when I saw my family walking beans that afternoon.

Excited for vastly different reasons, the boys and I joined the bean walkers. After walking one loop, I said, "Well, I have groceries in the car. I need to get going."

The boys wanted to stay. I drove away, knowing they would need to finish the field before Grandpa brought them home. My smile lasted the two-mile drive to Mom's. This wasn't a dairy barn where my sons could test that hip bump, but those were real weeds and corn that they were pulling and chopping from the bean field.

# Cream

For the first eighteen years of my life, I drank raw, whole, straight-from-the-cow milk. I remember pulling two-quart Tupperware pitchers from the fridge in the morning and being disgusted by one and a half inches of cream on the top. In eight hours, from barn in the evening to fridge in the morning, the fatty cream rose to the top. We would ladle it off and dump it down the drain. Every single chunky bit needed to be gone before my siblings and I would pour it over our cereal.

My opinion of cream has changed dramatically over time. Every day, I love an early morning cup of strong coffee. With a bit of added sweetness. And with a splash of half-and-half. And if by chance there is a small carton of heavy whipping cream in my fridge left over from cooking some thick pasta sauce or rich dessert, all the better.

When visiting Bill's family in England, I drink my coffee with thick English double cream. Just the thought of its decadence whets my taste buds. The most memorable coffee I've ever had was at Bill's mum's house in 1994. Under the morning summer sun, June's neighbors joined us on the cozy patio in her flower garden. We laughed and chatted over strong coffee that June had made in a French press. To mine, I added sugar and a big glug of English double cream. Double cream pours out of the tub the way thick crepe batter pours from a bowl. It falls into the black coffee, then rebounds up to float on the top.

In England, cigarette wrappers are prominently marked "SMOKING KILLS." I wonder how many more decades will pass before double cream, clotted cream, single cream, and various other full-fat cousins will have a similar warning.

In addition to floating on coffee, a drenching pour of double cream saturates most spoon-eaten English desserts such as trifle and Yule log. After twenty years of this decadence, I now try to get to the distribution point to stop this pour – with the exception of when traditional chocolate Yule log is served.

When I was growing up, Dad poured milk over every piece of cake I ever saw him eat, and as kids, my siblings and I used to break up graham crackers, sprinkle sugar on them, and reduce them to mush with milk. Then there is the famous cookie that loves milk, Oreos, which we sunk into tall glasses of milk for an after-school snack. This smothering of milk products over desserts was not as foreign to me as I initially thought when the cream flowed in England.

Then there's the ultra-indulgence of at least one cream tea whenever I go to England. It's debatable which is spread first on the scone, the sweet strawberry jam or generously portioned clotted cream, but either way, a cream tea is the combination of sweet and rich atop a fresh scone and accompanied by English tea.

Clotted cream originates from Devonshire in England. It spreads like butter. The most memorable cream tea I've ever had was next to a clapper bridge in Postbridge on the Dartmoor in Devon. Built in medieval times, clapper bridges dot the Dartmoor and give way over rivers and streams. These bridges, built in the thirteenth century, consist of three pillars of stacked stones with large slabs laid across the top to create the pass. The Dartmoor is the setting of *The Hound of the Baskervilles*, a Sherlock Holmes mystery written by Sir Arthur Conan Doyle. In a letter to his mother written in 1901, Doyle describes the large, unsettled, misty, barren land as "a great place, very sad & wild, dotted with the dwellings of prehistoric man, strange monoliths and huts and graves." A perfect place for this writer to submerse himself while writing a terrifying tale about a gigantic black dog that glowed in the dark.

Over a hundred years since Doyle visited, Dartmoor National Park covers just under 236,000 acres and is still England's largest open tract of wild land. Comparatively, Yellowstone National Park has over 2,000,000 acres of wilderness. The Dartmoor's official website promotes the area as having a "very gentle side" with "safe quiet areas" where "Dartmoor Ponies are an iconic sight, living as semi-wild herds all over the moor."

In 1994, the same year as that memorable coffee, Bill and I went to Devon for a week with his family. We stayed in a beautiful cottage within walking distance of a pub, and we spent a few days walking the moor. In the middle of the Dartmoor, we stopped one afternoon at the village store in Postbridge. The store was near a clapper bridge where scones and jam were served up on paper plates with tubs of clotted cream. A quarter pound of cream per person. This wasn't a formal or high tea at one of the many pubs and hotels dotting the fringes of the moor. Fortunately, as I sat down on a rock next to the clapper bridge, my tub rolled into the stream, so Bill and I shared one. An eighth of a pound per person still made for over a quarter-inch-thick layer of clotted cream on each of our scone halves.

Years ago, I browsed recipes trying to work out how clotted cream is made. I vaguely recall one recipe that suggested the first thing to do was to go to a local farm for fresh milk from Jersey cows – those cows that originate from the Isle of Jersey. Jersey milk has the highest percentage of fat content than any other cattle breed. I love it when a recipe is an adventure. Jersey is a Channel Island under the English crown but physically closer to France than England. It's just southwest of the Isle of Guernsey, another land of brown cows.

To make clotted cream? Someday. Probably not in Iowa. Most dairy cows I see there are black and white Holsteins. Probably not in England. I don't know any farmers there. Perhaps Vermont? Could I get fresh milk from Billings Farm & Museum, the oldest Jersey dairy farm in this country? Doubtful. It's highly unlikely to be handed a container of raw Jersey milk similar to those two-quart Tupperware containers we carried from barn to house twice daily when I grew up. The proposition of distributing raw milk frightens some people.

After our trips to England, I revert back to salads and fish, with rarely a dessert in the house. However, I still sip coffee with half-and-half every morning and hold tight to the vision of that rich double cream coffee with friends in June's sun-drenched garden – and to the wasted quarter pound of clotted cream floating down the stream under a clapper bridge.

# Fields of English Flowers

———◆———

At the end of May 2012, we were in England for Bill's mum's 80th birthday, which happened to coincide with Queen Elizabeth's Diamond Jubilee, the country's celebration of sixty years of the Queen's reign.

I was a little shocked during this visit to find no cream in the small English fridge when we arrived. Bill's family had been buying a lower-fat cream. It just didn't work for me. It was missing that soft, velvety thickness. In the Malcolm fridge in England, there was now a cream substitute. It can be purchased as a single cream or a double cream, but there is a dead giveaway that it's a fraud: it doesn't float to the top of the coffee when poured – at least the single version didn't when I poured it into my coffee. I read the ingredients and saw that it was lightened with added vegetable oil. I can't remember the exact number of grams of fat and what the serving size was, but this is an exaggerated, approximated ratio: 3,000 to 2,500. To which I ask, why bother? I'm not in England often. I bought real cream and allayed my guilt with an occasional walk.

Bill grew up in the town of Stevenage, Hertfordshire. Stevenage was the first "new town" designed to move people out of poor or bombed areas of London. Stevenage "Old Town" residents still consider this influx of Londoners as a rather unfortunate event. The village of Stevenage was straight north of London on the train line and was the first test of purposefully built "new towns" in 1946. Planners engulfed the village of Stevenage with an urban design of new homes in new neighborhoods with each having a community center, a pub, and small shops. The one nearest to the house where Bill grew up had a bakery, an Indian restaurant, and a small hardware store. Many of these neighborhood shops are now worn down.

Bill's family moved in the early 1990s to a relatively new housing estate on the outskirts of Stevenage. Just as Iowa fields are eaten up by housing, so were English fields in building this large tract of new homes. Bill's family's subdivision backs up to a lane leading to farm fields. Set up for a walking nation, or so it used to be, public footpaths meander throughout the countryside.

Out on a walk one afternoon, at the end of the lane and past a cluster of trees, I found a farm field that opened up like a solar glare on that cloudy English day. Occasionally seeing this crop covering rolling fields, I only knew it had the unfortunate name of "rape." I soaked up the color and snapped photos of the field and close-ups of individual plants with buttercup-yellow flowers. After this photographic outing, I tucked myself away in my bedroom overlooking June's garden and researched this crop. The name is derived from the Latin word *rapum*, which means *turnip*. In the UK, farmers use it as a winter "break crop," for it enhances the soil for the following rotation of wheat.

The leafy green stems shoot up spikes that blossom out buttercup flowers. Like pumpkins, strawberries, and soybeans, the flower matures and the "fruit" begins to grow. In this case, a pod of seeds forms and continues growing long after the flower has fallen off the end of it. The rape plants remind me of the cleomes in my flower garden as they share the same flowering and pod creation.

The raw oil from this crop, which is high in erucic acid, is used in industrial oils and lubricants. In the 1970s, through crossbreeding, Canadian scientists created a version of rape with low erucic acid and low glucosinolates, a Canadian low-acid oil suitable for human consumption and quite the hit due to being low in saturated fat. Now comes the puzzle. From that last sentence, can you piece together what this oil is called? Canola! (**Can**adian **l**ow **a**cid **o**il)

Throughout the holiday, I continued my occasional walks after coffee. Each time, the healthy cream and the real cream came to the table for coffee. Wanting to know what made this alternative cream healthier, one day I read the ingredients in depth to see exactly what constituted "vegetable oil." Rapeseed oil – canola oil – was one of the main ingredients. No wonder my taste buds rejected the lighter version.

I'm not overly interested in the ongoing disputes between real cream and this cream substitute. What I am certain of is that when in England, I want my English cream from those cows in the pasture, not from canola oil fields behind the house where I burn off some of those cream calories.

# At the Edge of a Memory

———◆———

Grandma Mills's orneriness drove us all a bit crazy at one point or another throughout her 89-year life. Few could argue that her spunk is what undoubtedly kept my dad's mother alive for so many years. In her mid-eighties, she fought hard to keep a leg that was slowly succumbing to poor circulation. Finally, she realized to get rid of the pain, the leg had to go. After she came out of surgery and recovery, she looked at me and said, "I haven't looked at it yet."

"Do you want to?" I asked.

She nodded.

I took the covers off so we could see her stump. Her leg had been amputated just above the knee. It was wrapped up meticulously in white gauze bandages. No sign of the pain she had endured for years. She looked down and said, "Aw hell, that ain't bad." This woman had been gored by a bull in '55, struck by lightning in '60 or '61, and poisoned by carbon monoxide from a furnace in '71. Her fingers had been mauled by an endgate seeder in '77. Neighbors attest that she worked harder than most men. She milked cows by hand and threw bales of hay to the rack as they came off the baler. She sweated. Looking at this pristine white bandage seemed tame. Her standard reply when asked how she was feeling was "Like I could kick the side out of hell!" I'm sure the devil flinched.

Her husband, my dad's father, Grandpa Mills, was nicknamed Scoop. According to Dad, the origins of this nickname came from Grandpa carrying a scoop shovel around with him whenever he was working outside. Dad asserted that he rarely used it, but rather he gave directions to everyone else on what needed to be done. Although unbearably gruff and at times downright scary, he had an occasional soft spot for his grandkids. When the smallest imperfection set him off, he could let loose a line of cussing and bellering that was simply unbelievable. Then, he wouldn't talk for a week or more.

My last memory of Grandpa Mills is from when I was nearly ten years old. Grandma Mills led me to his bedside, down the hallway of the mobile home they were living in while their farmhouse was being renovated. He didn't get out of bed to greet me. He looked at me and told me he was going to die. I thought how strange it was to be talking with him from this angle, with me looking down at him in bed. I had only known him standing up and filled with constant movement. I have no memories of him sitting. His fight was the first time I remember hearing the word *cancer*. His farmer gusto was no match for colon and pancreatic cancer, probably undiagnosed for years.

My mom's mother, Grandma Bauer, was my last living grandparent. She "went green" before it was the thing to do. She, like her mother, Great-Grandma Whittier, lived through the waste-not-want-not post–World War II generation. From the letters Grandma

Bauer sent to me over the years, I could publish quite a collection of recipes and pieces of advice – from how to remove a catsup stain to how to deal with cancer. She, too, was a breast cancer survivor. One letter that she wrote to me in July 2009, a month after I had been diagnosed, is on stationery with a collection of tiny songbirds and the words "Faith brings strength and hope." Inside she wrote this about her experience some twenty years earlier: "Well, I survived all that and am still kicking at 91 years. With age comes a lot of aches and pains, but they soon go away and don't develop into anything. I just enjoy the beautiful world. . . ." Grandma Bauer lived to be 95.

My mother's father, Granddad Bauer, was a man of few words and little cussing, at least none that I ever heard. Visually, I remember his huge smile and how laughing would make his whole face happy. His prayers before dinners are how I remember his voice. Granddad started grace the same way before every Sunday dinner, Christmas dinner, birthday dinner, and bullhead fish fry. While the prayer fit the occasion, to my ears it was always the same, perhaps more so in cadence than in words. I so wish I could remember the whole prayer. It was full of grace. One piece of his thanks-giving was something like "Bless the hands that prepared the food for the nourishment of our bodies."

While I remember these four grandparents fairly well, that's not the case for my great-grandma Whittier. From 1967 to 1968, the last two years in Great-Grandma Whittier's five-year diary, I find myself – "Kept Linda"

— a couple times a week. Each day's entry is on four narrow lines. I know that my great-grandma, who lived in Independence, Iowa, took care of me while Mom was out selling Avon. Our dairy farm was twelve miles from town, and there wasn't much of a market for Avon products with our Amish neighbors, hence these selling days in town.

I'm never the only recorded activity on any given day I was at Great-Grandma Whittier's. On August 12, 1968, she recorded, "Kept Linda. Helped Else look over 2 baskets of Swiss Chard. Got 60 ears of corn in freezer. Peeled a few apples."

I would've been two years old on this day. How did she accomplish so much? I was probably there only a few hours. Still, I confidently surmise that when I was at Great-Grandma's, I, too, looked over Swiss Chard, got corn in the freezer, and peeled a few apples. The abundance of produce in my childhood was as constant as the change of diapers on a baby.

My memories of Great-Grandma's house always start with the big black grate in the living room where warm air rose from the basement furnace in the winter. The grate was the size of an area rug, perhaps 8' x 10'. That was the measurement from a child's eyes; maybe it was really only 3' x 5'. It was big enough to make me, just a small kid, dread walking on it for fear I would fall through it to the basement. Some forty years later, I shudder walking over grates on sidewalks.

Great-Grandma's rocking chair sat at one end of the grate. It was an oversized wooden chair with a leather seat, probably more for Great-Grandpa, who had passed away, than Great-Grandma. She looked like a tiny Aunt Bea, complete with dress and apron. She kept a step stool next to the kitchen counter to reach the shelves in the upper cupboards. With her small frame and my child's frame, the two of us easily fit in that chair, with me on her lap. Firmly anchored there, I was okay at the edge of the grate – even bravely peeking into the depths of the basement below.

And that's where I lose the one detail I so wish I could completely remember. I know in that chair we either read books or looked at pictures in books. I know we looked at pictures of horses and cows for sale in the back of the *Wallaces Farmer* magazine. Yet, I'm convinced *Wallaces Farmer* is not where this near-memory lies. It's triggered by pictures, either paintings or photos, of horses or cows in a grassy pasture, at the end of a dirt lane, with a red barn in the background. Grandma must have read a farm book with me on her lap. The almost-memory is too ingrained to have been an image from browsing through a copy of *Wallaces Farmer*.

Sometimes after a night full of dreams, those visions won't come into focus the next day. The near-vision lingers in the subconscious, but when the brain turns to look directly at it, the shadow of the dream disappears. As if it's in the same room, only standing behind a door, refusing to come out into the open. That's where this near-memory stays.

I vividly remember details about Great-Grandma's house: the worn shoebox full of toys under the china closet, including an old metal toy phone; the graham crackers and fig cookies she kept in the storage drawer beneath the oven. Every great-grandchild had access to that drawer. I do not remember her voice, only the sound of her dentures clicking. I remember the big rubber tree plants and Christmas cacti on her front porch in the summertime. We entered her house through the back-porch door and into her kitchen; the living room was next to that. Even in summer months, I tiptoed around that ever-present grate as if a baleen whale's body lurked below, ready to suck me, a little plankton, right through the grill.

When seeking the source of this elusive dreamlike memory that leaves me with a fleeting warmth, I visually walk through the house again and again, thinking I just might bump into it. I reread Grandma's diary hoping to find a reference to what we read together, such as "Read *Little Farm* book to Linda." But there is no more than "Kept Linda." Forty years of wandering has only left me at the edge of a memory, exactly where I started.

# Morels

While visiting my family in Iowa in April 2012, I decided to go for a short walk on the gravel roads to my Amish friend Clara's house. I was preparing for a twenty-six-mile walk that May, the Avon Walk. Donations I collected would fund breast cancer research. This walk in the country was just a two-mile round trip. Clara's family lived next to Grandma Mills's farm. Clara and I were close in age and had remotely known of each other growing up, but we had become friends over the last couple of years when our paths crossed in that we both had gone through breast cancer around the same time.

In a short two or three minutes from Mom and Dad's, I passed their neighbors' house. Herbert came out to the road to say hello. I had babysat for his five kids when I was in high school. We'd known each other for a long time. He asked why I was carrying two cornstalks. When I told him it was to keep the mean country dogs from biting me, he raised an eyebrow. He can raise one eyebrow higher than anyone I've ever met.

"Come here. Take this," Herbert said. I had deliberately not picked up a stick, thinking that would be too heavy. "It's hickory. It's not heavy. You'll need it for the house on the corner." It was lighter than my two cornstalks combined.

Herbert walked down the road with me. I explained I would be walking in the Avon Walk Boston in May and was putting in a few miles while visiting Mom and Dad.

"Hmm. I walked two miles yesterday. Picked morels." He was gloating.

I could smell morels frying at the mention of their name. Dad had brought a few home from his travels earlier in the week, and Mom had fried them in flour and butter. We each had a tiny serving. An appetizer. A tease.

For those unfamiliar with morel mushrooms, they have a relatively short season and look like elongated, rounded, tan sponges standing upright on sturdy pedestals. Morels need moisture and then heat to make them push through grass and leaves. Top to bottom, they can be as tall as an adult's hand. Fresh mushrooms are like a clean cream-colored sponge. When they are a few days old, they begin to darken as they dry out. They are earthy tasting and pretty common in Iowa, but you have to know where to look for them. The theories of where to hunt mushrooms are many. Perhaps at the roots of elm trees. Or under old logs. I think some people can sense them, much like Dad can take two sticks and find water underground.

Any timberland with grazing cattle won't have them, for cows enjoy them as much as Iowans do. Morels sell for $40 or more a pound. No one I know sells them. They clean them, dip them in flour, fry them in butter, and eat them.

Salivating at Herb's mention of morels, I say, "Where?" A question no morel mushroom hunter answers. The one-word question just tumbled out of my mouth.

"In our timber."

Right next to the field where I had been cultivating the day before. (Set on not being wholly defined as a city girl, I had offered to chisel plow: to drive a big tractor with a plow towed behind it that broke up the ground in preparation for spring planting.)

"Oh," I replied, wondering if I could sneak in and pick just a few.

"We must have gotten four pounds yesterday. But there were snakes everywhere. Little baby ones."

"Oh . . ." Eighty percent chance this was a bluff. Morel Mushroom Territory Protection Strategy. "Just little garters?"

"No. Some other kind."

"Rat?"

"No."

"Corn?"

"No. Fox, I think."

I had never heard of a fox snake. Ninety percent chance this was a bluff.

"I know what you're doing. You're just telling me there are snakes so I won't touch your mushrooms!"

"Noooo! I wouldn't do that." Herbert's eyebrow shot up again. "I'm not kidding. There were snakes all over the place."

He seemed honest, sincere. Still, 70 percent chance this was a bluff.

We parted ways after a quarter mile. Herb returned home, and I continued to Clara's. On the way, I met the three dogs on the corner. They rushed to the road, barking angrily. I held the stick and the cornstalks high and shouted, "Stay!" They stopped.

Back at home, I told Mom about my encounter with Herbert. She laughed – 99 percent sure it was a bluff.

Snakes make me scream. I could not go morel hunting to prove Herbert right or wrong. Not with the possibility of barging in on a snake family.

That afternoon, Mom and I took the boys to Fontana Park, a small wildlife exhibit near Hazleton, Iowa, where all the animals on display are native to Iowa and are there because they were orphaned, injured, or human raised. In the visitors' center, there it was, slithering in a large aquarium tank. A fox snake. It emits a smell like a fox to ward off enemies, much like a skunk. The sign describing fox snakes said nothing about their ability to guard patches of morel mushrooms, nestled in amongst bluebells, jack-in-the-pulpits, ground ginger, and plants that look like little beach umbrellas. This snake was at least three feet long. I had no regrets about not calling Herbert's bluff on the guard snakes.

# Wandering through Pastures

Drunk drivers, racists, and Holstein bulls scare me. It's the uncertainty of their actions that leads me to impart the most conservative conflict management style: avoidance.

Growing up on a dairy farm, I had the words "Stay away from the bull pen!" drilled into my young rural soul. We had Holstein cattle, the breed that gives the most milk compared to any other. I remember those cows, especially the older ones, as big, cud-chewing, gentle bovine. During the summer, when I was in the barn at milk time, I would hold the cows' tails as Mom put the milking machines on each cow. That way she wouldn't get switched by the flick of a stringy tail. The tails moved like whips, and the hair at the end smarted if it made contact with your face.

Now, Mom and Dad are beef farmers, so the Holstein bull has been replaced by an Angus. Any bull can be mean, so now it's me who yells, "Stay away from the bull pen!" as Will and Liam go outside to play at the farm.

Since Holsteins are milk cows, they have regular and close relationships with farmers from the time they are calves. When we had a dairy farm with about seventy Holsteins, the calves were separated from the cows immediately after they were born. Then the fresh cows were milked, and the calves were bottle-fed the colostrum for a couple weeks. After that, the cows' regular milk would come in. For about six weeks, the calves were bottle-fed until they could belly up to the bunk and eat grain — a little shelled corn and oats, plus hay and a sprinkling of protein. Here, apparently, is where the problem starts with Holstein bulls. As kids, when we bottle-fed the calves, we would pet the cowlicks twirling in the middle of their foreheads and even let the calves suck on our fingers.

Unlike dogs, which need to be socialized with humans early on to be good pets, socialization with bulls creates *too much* of a human comfort level. As the bull calves age, twice-daily bottle feedings make them less shy around humans, and they start to identify humans as their own kind. Plus, rubbing their foreheads makes them more prone to head-butting, a precursor to aggression. In instances where cows should shy away from humans — the way the beef cattle do when we drive the Ranger to the timber — bottle-fed bulls don't back down or move away. And when a one-ton, six-foot-tall bull has no fear, he struts it. He wasn't afraid of anyone when he was a calf, and he knows he doesn't need to be now at 2,000 pounds.

In cartoons, bulls paw and snort and then, if mad enough, charge. The pawing and snorting are true enough, but another behavior is more chilling. When threatened, bulls stand sideways to show the other animal or human their full breadth of power. They keep an eye on the troublemaker without turning their head toward the subject. With exceptional peripheral vision, an angry bull bulges his eyes and sees everything but his own rear end. If that animal or human doesn't slowly retreat beyond twenty feet, a bull will most likely charge. The estimate of twenty feet is the fight-or-flight boundary.

So much for the cute black and white fuzzy calves. And what kid who grew up on a dairy farm didn't pet these spring packages on the head? Little did we know that this closeness would create a later fierceness. Had the Holstein bull that cornered and gored Grandma Mills on a feed lot in 1970 been a sweet, coddled calf? She recovered from the incident, and her experience precipitated the warning "Stay away from the bull pen!"

Speaking of bulls, I'm reminded of an idyllic public footpath in England. These pathways crisscross the countryside, right through private property – farms and fields. On one of my first visits to see my husband Bill's family, we were on a walk in the country with his mum, June, leading the way. I stopped short on one side of a fence that his mum was about to cross. On the other side of the fence, I saw a young bull across the field. I calmly and robotically recited the ingrained warning "That's a bull; we shouldn't be in a field with a bull."

Having navigated public footpaths for many years, June assured me that we would be fine. We climbed over a stile – think of a waist-high wooden fence with step stools on either side – and I took it upon myself to put a watchful eye on the young bull. No more story to tell, for that bull paid no attention to us walkers.

Only cream teas rank higher than public footpaths in my list of English favorites. Farmers are required by the government to keep these paths passable and a meter wide, to mow them, to trim overhanging trees, not to plow them up – let alone set up any man-made obstacle. And, according to the English government's website, obstructing a pathway is a criminal offense. That made me think about the bull situation.

Are English bulls simply more proper than American breeds? English docility had been my justification for that bull's behavior for many years. However, a quick read on the English government's website revealed why that bull was in the field. It was less than ten months old and not a British Holstein – or any of six other banned dairy breeds. It's a criminal offense to keep mature Holstein bulls in fields containing public footpaths.

There it is, set forth in an English law: justification for my ever-skyrocketing anxiety near bull pens in Iowa.

# Black Dirt

I miss good black dirt. Our house and the whole town, if not the state of Massachusetts, is built on ledge – big rocks. These make for spectacular cliffs but are not great for planting flowers. Throughout town, big pieces of ledge have been blasted to make room for houses. A new house in our area sits six feet from a newly blasted rocky cliff. No backyard. Just a back rock.

We have muckish-colored dirt that's filled with broken glass. Apparently, years ago, our property was a dump for glass bottles. We have a ridge of maple trees all around our property. When the boys were little, they loved climbing up the hill and hiding in the trees. But every spring before the leaves popped, I searched the hill for glass brought to the surface by the spring thaw. I spent hours picking up broken glass so it didn't end up in a little boy's hand.

In 2005, the year we moved to Massachusetts, I decided to create a small flower garden at the bottom of the ridge. I took a spade to my pathetic-looking dirt and slowly turned it over, revealing rocks and glass with every twist of the shovel. Occasionally, I struck a rock that would jar me to the core, much like Wile E. Coyote when he continually smacked into a brick wall while chasing the Road Runner.

In 1991, when Bill and I bought our first house in Rockford, Illinois, I planted perennial flowers. At first I had a small garden behind our house, but after mowing and scalping a 30-foot-long gently sloping hill next to my new flower garden for two years, I knew something had to change. I had a vision for a bigger flower garden. Instead of scalping the hill every time I mowed, I was going to plow it up. Mom and Dad gave me a tiller for my birthday, and Bill went to work, pushing the tiller and ripping up the sod. After I got the grass chunks killed off, I started planting. Coneflowers, Shasta daisies, goosenecks, buttercups, phlox – anything I put in the ground grew in my sun-drenched rich Midwestern soil. When we moved from that house fourteen years later, the flowers were firmly established and more than waist-high. Glorious, just like a thickly growing English country garden.

Then we moved to New England, where I had only four-inch-deep, rock-filled, glass-filled, shade-filled, pitiful dirt.

My friend Kim has created the most spectacular garden over the last fifteen years. I imagine that having grown up in Michigan, she, too, was used to good dirt. Her garden was a paved drive when she bought her house. She had the asphalt jackhammered out and then went about creating, encouraging, and feeding the ground. The result is breathtaking. And she continuously nurtures her dirt, sometimes bringing in horse manure and occasionally collecting droppings from a friend's rabbit.

So as I bemoaned my rock-filled earth, I had a vision of a clear Iowa cornfield ready for spring planting. Just a field of smooth black dirt. Yet my mind flashed back to a scene from my childhood. I knew why there were no rocks in those fields. I was probably around ten years old when Dad pulled a hayrack behind a tractor while Mom, Grandma Mills, and us kids picked up rocks and chucked them on the rack. For years, freshly turned earth revealed new rocks that had to be removed before planting corn and beans. My annual spring glass collection had pulled memory strings from those days picking up rocks to create smooth fields.

A couple of years ago, I found a gem on our property. Next to our barn and outside the fence around our backyard, I knocked down a weedy mess so I could plant a red climbing rosebush against the barn's old stone wall. Surrounded by maple trees that were fully leafed out and bordered by the fence, this 20 x 20-foot spot had the makings of a secret garden. My shovel slid through that dirt as if the ground were a devil's food chocolate cake made fresh from Mom's Betty Crocker cookbook. This little piece of our land had been ignored for years before we moved in. Leaves fell and were never raked. Vegetation was left to die down and rot back into the ground. The richness of decay here mimicked that of the Midwest prairie where the prairie grass life cycle pushed nutrients back into the earth year after year before the settlers began farming the land in swaths of fields. For this little piece of Massachusetts, a decade of decaying leaves made the ground look and feel like a little bit of Iowa.

Regardless of whether the soil beneath my feet is Iowa rich or Massachusetts ledge, it still makes for good summer dirt. I love summer dirt more than I love summer. Summer dirt used to tattoo my little boys with a day's play. As they ran with their friends between the sprinkler and the fort, jumping on the trampoline and crawling underneath it, those dirty kids were summer's best. The boys started the days freshly laundered, and by sundown, they were a mess, some of the happiest little messes ever. They were streaked with sweat and water, covered in dirt, and exhausted. I looked at them and thought of my own childhood. The one mark of summer I best remember was seeing a trace of watermelon juice running down my inner arms, creating a dried riverbed and contrasting the day's dirt adhesion with slightly cleaner skin created by the juice river.

"Why do I need to take a shower?" my son asked.

Because now I'm the mom who washes the sheets. And I remember the days when my mom with four kids didn't always make us take showers, but she made us at least wash the riverbeds from our arms and the black dirt from our feet.

# Iowa Storms

The summer of 2017, I was in Iowa on our annual summer escape from the Northeast. For a couple weeks each year, I take the boys back to the Midwest to visit cousins, Grandpa, Grandma, aunts, and uncles. My husband, Bill, usually joins us for a long weekend over the Fourth of July.

On this trip, we had storms two of the three days we were visiting my sister in southern Iowa. My sister's house sits atop a hill, so there is a clear 360-degree view of the sky. If there was a tornado, you would see it coming – unless it dropped from an air collision directly above the house.

Seeing black waves rolling across the sky makes me shake. Heavy humidity combined with anticipatory stillness. Uncertainty of the oncoming wind. On that Saturday, there were no tornado warnings, only thunderstorm warnings, and a tornado watch until 11 p.m. To me, thunderstorm warnings mean imminent thunder, lightning, wind, and heavy rain – but little chance of swirling clouds.

Back at Mom and Dad's a few days later, we watched more storms scream across the radar on TV during a special weather bulletin. In an hour or so it would pass, said the female meteorologist in an assertive tone. She directed viewers in this storm's path to take cover. Avoid interior western walls. Avoid windows. Ten miles from us, where my brother and his family live, 93 mph winds had been reported.

This storm took on a new dimension – not a tornado but a derecho, a straight-line wind storm. The word is Spanish for *straight* and is pronounced də-ˈrā-(ˌ)chō. This rarity produces wind gusts of a Category 1 hurricane and is often accompanied by hail up to two inches in diameter. No spinning, just a huge mass of angry clouds making a mad sprint across the prairie skies.

I don't recall derechos when I was growing up. Perhaps more high-tech meteorological tools can identify and track these high-end storms. They can now predict down to the minute when communities will feel the impact of storms. That certainty didn't exist thirty years ago. Back then, as we watched a breaking weather report on TV, a red tornado warning would cover an entire county, and we'd head for the basement. And wait. When it blew over, we'd come up and look for damage.

In town, sirens sound as a warning for residents to take cover. During one of these storms in the 1980s, Mom and I had just stopped in to see Aunt Helen. Uncle Lee was out with the volunteer fire department, watching the skyline for storms. He was an early-day storm chaser. Our nearly five-foot-tall aunt held a radio and listened to the dispatches between firefighters. We walked into her house, and with radio in hand, Aunt Helen immediately ushered us to her basement. I remember the event being more humorous than scary. Aunt Helen wedged the three of us into a shower stall for a good twenty minutes. At home, we would have been playing pool in the basement, away from windows.

Despite the storms throughout the week at my sister's, the heat and humidity remained high – until the third morning. We woke up to clear sunny skies, and a barefoot step outside the back door landed on cool concrete. There hadn't been a storm overnight, but the humidity had broken and the temperature had dropped. The calmness of that change reminded me of New England. Since we moved here in 2005, fierce humidity in the air can be cleared by a polite, steady wind from inland to the coast. The temperature can drop in minutes. No thunder. No storm. No derecho.

For days in New England, we watch the approach of nor'easters or hurricanes. Thankfully, we live in a town several miles from the coast, so we have only been in the outer circles of the hurricanes, feeling moderate bands of wind and rain but no swelling, crashing waves flooding our streets. The nor'easters' spigots may turn on and hover over us for days, dropping feet of snow or inches of rain. Neither of these New England weather events unsettles me like angry, unpredictable storms steaming across the wide-open Midwestern sky.

# Carbs! Glorious Carbs!

In 2017, I spent our seventeen-day summer excursion in Iowa mostly barefoot. On grass. In water. Around a campfire. Across gravel. My decisions about where to go and whom to see were guided predominantly by whether or not I had to put shoes on. One day during our stay at Mom and Dad's, Liam headed out the door barefoot. I asked him where his shoes were. He asked why I wanted to know, and he was right. Playing outside at Grandma and Grandpa's, it didn't really matter where his shoes were. Indeed, why was I asking?

A vacation in Iowa means a switch to a shoeless culture reminiscent of my childhood. And it doesn't stop there. Normally more resistant to carbs, on this trip I gave in to those as readily as I went barefoot. Nothing is easier than putting meat between two slices of bread for a quick lunch. And as for a bacon and catsup sandwich on white bread for breakfast, well, at least I skipped the accompanying pancakes.

Living on a farm means nearly nonstop movement year round. Planting and harvesting in the fields and the gardens. Planting flowers and pulling weeds all season. Daily feeding of cattle and checking on them in the timber. Carbs fuel this life, giving the energy to thrive.

One Sunday afternoon, we were heading to a potluck dinner reunion at Fontana Park for my mom's side of the family. Liam had discovered Hawaiian rolls at my sister's house during the first couple days of our trip. Those sweet, soft, buttery dinner rolls are a mystery to many New Englanders, much as fresh steamed lobster is to Iowans. Liam loved these rolls, so I asked one of my aunts if she would pick some up on her way through town.

A few days earlier, Mom and I let everyone know that we would bring scalloped potatoes and ham, fruit, veggies, and peanut butter and jelly sandwiches. For good measure, we threw in sliced turkey and ham. There were twelve picnic tables in the covered shelter at the park. We set up a table for desserts and another one with an inflatable plastic "cold island" with ice in it to keep fruits, veggies, sliced meats, and deviled eggs cold. On the table closest to the electrical outlet, we plugged in the Crock-Pot of scalloped potatoes and ham. On another table, we put out a loaf of wheat bread with chunky peanut butter and strawberry jam.

The carb table was a little sparse and pitiful – until everyone started arriving . . . with rolls! The turkey and ham sandwiches suddenly had more bread choices than a Hawaiian sweet roll or a flimsy slice of wheat bread. I remember the full table but not all the varieties . . . with one exception – my aunt brought her famous homemade rolls "because that was the easiest thing I could make." I know no one else who would let those words flow so easily over her lips. Her rolls were still warm, and butter melted so beautifully on my split roll that I ate it without any meat. The first one, that is.

Desserts that day – brownies and chocolate chip cookies – joined forces with all sorts of sweets over the course of seventeen days: my aunt's homemade apple, blackberry, and chocolate pies; a standard Iowa 9" x 13" pan of cinnamon rolls from an Amish friend as a thank-you to Mom and Dad for a favor – with a loaf of homemade bread on the side; Mom's chocolate drop and chocolate chip cookies, perfectly baked; and monster cookies from Liam's hero, dubbed "Monster Cookie Girl." She is a neighbor of Mom and Dad's who brought monster cookies to their house when we were visiting over a year ago.

During our vacation on the farm, Mom grilled steaks and chicken. She had baked potatoes, boiled potatoes, mashed potatoes, or leftover scalloped potatoes on the side for every meal. When we first arrived home, the table was set for fourteen for supper. Served family style, the bowls and plates of food just kept going round and round the table. The only food missing at that dinner was just-picked corn on the cob. We were a month too early for Mom and Dad's fresh corn. I passed on vegetable seconds, except for what was nearly not a vegetable – potatoes.

Boiled and mashed spuds remind me of my grandpas on either side of the family. Potatoes were a supper staple for those two farmers. Sitting at that table with potatoes on my plate, it was a strange way to feel close to those who are no longer with us. But potatoes can pull my memories of my grandpas so close to the present that it makes my eyes water.

With my shoes back on in Boston and no cattle to take care of, I went back to watching carbs. I knew I had let myself overindulge in carbs way more than normal during those seventeen days. I know that I can't bake every week or keep lovely fresh loaves of bread on my kitchen counter. For some days, my energy exertion is only a walk to the car, then a walk into the library.

With fewer carbs converting to sugar, my body was in withdrawal the first few days back in Massachusetts. While they tasted good going over the tongue, those carbs landed in places that made the waistband on my shorts difficult to connect. Once back home, I kicked my shoes off under the library table where I was writing and made a mental plan for my midday meal. I would have a salad for lunch, without croutons.

# Roasted Potatoes

———◆———

Regularly a part of an English roast dinner, roasted potatoes are crackly and perfectly browned on the outside and soft on the inside. I make roasted vegetables at home. I collect a variety of hardy root vegetables such as potatoes, sweet potatoes, carrots, and parsnips. Then I cube them into my big 1960s barely yellow mixing bowl, drizzle enough olive oil to cover them, add salt and pepper – and maybe a little fresh chopped rosemary – and roast them in a 400-degree oven. After fifteen minutes, I flip them so they roast evenly. They are good, but they never come out with that great English crunch covering.

While in England one year for an unusual Thanksgiving visit, I was keeping Bill's sister, Anne, company in the kitchen while she was making dinner: steak and kidney pie (steak and mushroom for me), roasted potatoes and parsnips, boiled carrots, green beans, and gravy. We were just waiting for the roasted potatoes. I hadn't seen the beginning of the process, so I asked Anne exactly what she had done. Anne explained that she had peeled the potatoes, cut them in half, and parboiled them for five minutes. Then she put them in the roasting pan and covered them with fat. I hovered to watch the roasting process, looking for the secret of why mine weren't English.

After several minutes in the oven, Anne checked on them. She pulled the pan out, tilted it to one side, and spooned fat from the gully at the bottom of the pan over the potatoes.

Stateside problem #1: I never use that much oil.

We had a brief chat about the difficulty of really getting the potatoes roasted properly because there is usually something else in the oven that can't take the temperature that proper roasted vegetables need. Perhaps I could make pot roast in the Crock-Pot and roasted veggies in the oven?

I glanced at the counter and saw an open empty can. Anne's eyes followed my gaze.

"Ahhh, and that is supposed to be the very best for roasted veg – goose fat." A whole ten-ounce can of goose fat was crisping up those spuds in the oven.

Stateside problem #2: No cans of goose fat at my grocery store. And if goose fat is sold anywhere near me, I'm better off not knowing where.

I had an extra helping of Anne's English roasted potatoes that night, knowing I wouldn't replicate them at home.

# Baby Chicks

With downy yellow feathers, chicks are absolutely adorable. When I was a kid, each spring Mom bought around a hundred baby chicks, and we kids would help get them settled. We would lift each one out of the crate and gently dip its beak in the water so it would know where to find a drink on its own. Mom would use a foot-high ring from a hog feeder as a fence to keep them in one area of the back part of the old corncrib that we used as a baby chicken house. Mom hung a heat lamp over the top of it to keep the chicks warm. Tiny, tiny, tiny little chirps would fill the air as they made the transition to their new home. Then they nestled together under the heat lamp, looking like a big fuzzy sun. Once the chicks were cozied up, the chirping started to subside as they felt the warmth from the light and from one another's little winged bodies.

On cool spring mornings when we went in to feed them, the chirping would start as the first crack of sunlight hit their eyes and they heard the door creak open. Stepping over the fence, we would take ground corn in to fill the feeders. The chicks would see our toes and start pecking at them, not enough to really hurt, just enough to keep us on edge of that eventual one peck that would make a little red mark. That first strong peck was an indicator that we would need to guard our feet better in the future.

When the chicks feathered out, we would put them in the chicken coop. It had a big outside fenced area attached to it. Their food and water were outside. When they were young, the chicks had only the coop and the fenced area in which to wander. They needed to learn this was home, where it was safe to sleep at night. If they didn't learn this lesson and decided to find their own roost for the night, they would be open prey for skunks, raccoons, and possums. When they got bigger, we would open the chicken coop doors every morning so they could roam around for the day, scratching for bugs and looking for loose corn kernels around the grain bins. These were free-range chickens.

Around dusk, their homing mechanism would kick in, and they would return to the safety of the chicken coop. Once they were all quietly on roosts, Mom would close the door to the coop, making it secure so that it did not become a midnight meal house for those predators that, if given the chance, could wipe out all the birds in one night.

Hens would start laying eggs when they were six to eight months old. Picking up eggs was one of my favorite jobs. The nest stand was made of metal and looked a bit like a honeycomb. It had eight sixteen-inch-wide nests, four across and two high, with boards as roosts on the outside of each entrance. Hens would pick a straw-filled hole, hop inside, lay eggs, and then leave. But not the "setters." They were tough old ladies, unwilling to freely relinquish their eggs. I would wear gloves to protect my hands from their vicious pecks. From twenty chickens, we would get fifteen to nineteen eggs a day.

One of my first pets was a little chick that I got for Easter when I was five years old. Starting off downy yellow, she grew up to have red feathers, so I named her Red. (We also had a dog we called Dog.) I would pull an ear of corn out of the corncrib and walk around the barnyard rolling kernels of corn off the ear while Red and the other chickens followed me around, snatching up what I dropped. And that's about all you can do with a pet chicken. I think she lived for five years. When I was around ten years old, I went in and found her in the roost, head down, eyes closed. I so hoped she was just asleep. I tore out of the chicken house in tears. I seem to recall her and my Grandpa Mills's passing to be close. Dad buried her out by the cornfield, and we put a cement block on her grave with a plastic red rose. Although just a chicken, I imagine the block is still there marking Red's grave in our little overgrown pet cemetery, where five dogs and a cat are also buried.

# A Fowl Story

———◆———

"Playdate" was not a part of my family's vocabulary when I was a kid. The closest thing we ever had to a playdate was when my mom and my aunt got together in late summer, once at our house and once at their house, to butcher chickens. My lack of interest in cooking whole fowl most likely stems from those butchering days.

(An aside: as a favor to a friend, who is a longtime dedicated reader of my essays, I plant this warning: Move along to the next essay *now* if you don't want to know how your bag of frozen chicken breasts comes to be.)

As my mom and my aunt quickly cut the heads off of twenty chickens with a butcher knife, they would let those flip-flapping bodies loose onto the ground. Even without eyes, headless chickens can chase nine kids with incredible accuracy. The safest place to run was to the back of the pickup truck. Barefooted, we flew across the gravel driveway to clamber up the bumper and over the tailgate.

Once the chickens were still, Mom and my aunt brought out big pots of boiling water and poured it into two five-gallon buckets. They dipped the chickens into the scalding water to loosen the feathers. Then each of us kids had work to do . . . plucking feathers. The soft feathers were easiest to pull out. The wings were the toughest. The youngest kids pulled the easy ones, and then the oldest kids and our moms had to clean up what the five-year-olds left on each chicken. As we worked, the boy cousins tried to whack us girls on our bare legs with a dead chicken. We choreographed our own chicken dance to avoid contact.

While Mom built a fire in the 55-gallon trash barrel, where we normally burned garbage from the house, my aunt would oversee the plucking. After we plucked, my mom and my aunt would hold the naked chickens over the flames to singe off all the tiny pin feathers and hair. That ended the work of the kids, and we were free to play outside.

I distinctly remember the chicken kitchens of my youth. Whether butchering at our house or at my aunt's, kitchens became processing plants on butchering day. No meals would be made in the kitchen for us while my mom and aunt worked. Instead, earlier in the day, they made cold sandwiches and baked goodies that we ate outside, away from the activity in the kitchen.

The chickens were gutted and rinsed in the sink, moved to the table or counter, cut up into pieces, and put into Cryovac bags with twist ties. The smell of those plastic bags in bulk pervaded the kitchen whenever it was time to freeze food. Granddad Bauer worked at Cryovac in Cedar Rapids, and he would bring home reject bags for freezing food. I don't think we ever bought a single freezer bag from the store. Strangely, the smell memory of those bags lingers more vividly than that of the chickens.

Chickens, twenty of them. Forty drumsticks, thighs, and wings; twenty unsplit chicken breasts, hearts, livers, and gizzards. No boning or skinning. With all this activity and the high quantity of chicken parts, the newspapers on the kitchen floor were soon soaked in splattered chicken juice. With the kitchen near the back door at both our house and my aunt's house, the cousins – all nine of us – would whirl through, backwards and forwards, as our moms worked. Our moms would yell, "Get out of here! Go outside!"

But the bathrooms were inside. In both houses, the bathrooms were through the living rooms, and the living rooms were connected to the kitchens. Of course, we were barefoot. Surely our immune systems were strengthened each summer, considering where that chicken juice ended up. It was well distributed by eighteen little feet.

At my aunt's house one year, one of those boy cousins planted a big dead bull snake on the doorstep of his house. He had hoped his sister would step on it. That black thing all neatly coiled up was more the size of a small python than a garter snake. My mom, carrying a big tray of bagged chickens to the truck, walked out of the house and stepped on it with her bare feet. She screamed but held on to the tray of chickens. My cousin was mortified when my mom – not his sister – stepped on it! My aunt took off chasing and cussing my cousin. I didn't know aunts could move that fast.

The twenty chickens butchered in a day would not even make a dent in Mom's freezer space. I think a small cow could fit in each of her freezers. Every time I go home, the freezers seem to grow in enormity. There are three of them in the basement, referred to as the freezer on the west wall, the freezer on the south wall under the stairs, and the freezer on the south wall against the west wall. Mom has a running catalog in her head as to what is in each freezer, and each one is nearly full.

Mom and Dad gave Bill and me a small deep freeze as a wedding gift. After a trip home to Mom and Dad's, I think of my baby freezer as an offspring of theirs. Comparing the contents of our freezers, I see the different path I've taken in life. Away from the farm. Away from the meat locker. Mom and Dad rarely buy beef and pork at the store. They buy a pig from their neighbor and fill their freezer with beef from cattle they've raised. Their freezer is filled with neatly wrapped white packages of meat processed at the locker, no per-pound cost listed on each package. I feel I have to pay for all my meat twice: once at the grocery store and again when I see the price on the package when it comes out of the freezer.

What I rarely see in Mom's freezer are whole chickens and bone-in chicken parts. I'm guessing Mom, like me, got more than her fill of whole fowl during those years. I know exactly where my bag of individually frozen chicken breasts is, and I bet Mom knows which freezer her chicken breasts are in as well.

I know all too well that "butchering chickens" was from a different place and time – a different era – and ridiculously foreign to my little family in New England.

One morning a few years ago, I asked my ten-year-old son, Liam, to take out the recycling, and his finger got wet from rinse water on the garbage bag. Oh, the ire. And seeing his older brother Will in a chicken kitchen is unfathomable. Will puffs up with pride about his summer feet as he walks across the paved driveway barefoot. "I can walk on anything with my bare feet. They are so indestructible!"

I chuckle.

On a hot, humid, icky Massachusetts summer day, I went out to water the flower baskets on my deck. Just when I thought my outdoor chore was done, I saw a dead rabbit between the trampoline and the swing set. I inspected it, then thought I'd get Bill to clean it up. However, a thought struck me as abruptly as if I had stepped on the tines of a rake and gotten knocked in the head by the handle. Bill, too, has never been in a chicken kitchen. Really, the one with the most credentials to take care of this job was me.

I scooped up the carcass with a shovel and tossed it out behind the barn. I looked at the spot where I'd found the rabbit – where my hillbilly son runs barefoot – and there was no evidence of this circle of life event. Still, I got bleach water and poured it over the ground. I'm sure Mom and my aunt bleached the kitchen floor after their circle of life event, too.

# Roosters

I once asked my mom what useful purpose roosters served on the farm. She immediately started laughing, saying, "Linda, surely you know what roosters do!!!" That put both of us on the floor laughing.

"Of course I do! But we never hatched our own chicks, so why did we have roosters around?"

I asked because the rooster I so vividly recall was the meanest damn bird. To avoid attack when we left the house, we kept a long-handled spade outside by the door to hold him off so we could make it to the truck. If he was super aggressive, we'd use it to knock him a bit silly.

That rooster terrified us kids. We would carefully open the back door, peek out, and grope for the handle of the spade leaning against the side of the house. Often, hearing the door open would bring him running, full strut. An alpha male, he had no fear even though he was only a third the size of a kid. Honestly, I can't remember what color his feathers were. I only remember his running gait and seeing that head bobbing back and forth. His pace never slowed when the spade was in sight. He was brazen and bold, but dumb.

In the morning, when we walked down our long lane to wait for the school bus, that rooster would sometimes find us. Our screams would draw Mom out of the house, and she would act as a decoy and get him to chase her instead of us.

So why did we have that rooster? I had forgotten that we had taken him in when Mom's cousin and her family moved away to Missouri and could not take him with them. We were a rooster refuge. Neither Mom nor I can remember whatever happened to him, but we both remember his mean streak.

Another rooster troubled my family long before any farm memories settled into my brain. When Mom and Dad were first married, my dad had a "pet" rooster with enormous spurs on the back of his legs near his feet. When Grandma Mills or Mom went into the chicken coop to pick up eggs, the rooster often saw their visits as an opportunity for battle. He would jump on their backs and peck them, using those spurs to dig in. I can easily visualize the episode, complete with the soundbite of the cussing that ensued. One day after my grandma had been attacked, my mom told Grandma they had a little job to do. The rooster had chosen the wrong day for battle because Mom and Grandma had extra time on their hands.

It took Dad a while to realize the rooster was gone. When he finally asked about him, Mom simply said, "You ate him for dinner a few days ago."

I hesitate to write this. To hear this story without the background of living in a place so close to your meals, it sounds barbaric. Yet, over thirty-five years later, we all laugh over it. Dad says he didn't eat chicken for a month after that. And the reason that rooster was kept around? Dad and Grandpa liked to hear him crow. Guess who never picked up the eggs?

# Skunks

———◆◆◆———

Growing up as the oldest of four on a dairy farm, I held down the fort in the house while Mom milked cows morning and night. Dad worked second shift at a meat processing plant so that we could survive on the farm, which usually left Mom with the twice-daily milking of our small twenty-head Holstein herd. Watching my siblings must have been uneventful since I don't have any significant memories of them; however, I do remember wild animals in the house.

The first incident was when I was around ten years old. One evening, my sister and I saw a mouse run along a wall in the kitchen. After some high-pitched screaming, we decided to take care of it before Mom came in from milking the cows, for we couldn't stand the thought of the rodent running around for another hour. We found a snap trap, put some cheese on it, set it, and pushed it near the mouse path. We moved to the mouse-free living room and waited – half hoping nothing would happen until Mom came into the house. But there it was . . . SNAP! We flew to the kitchen and immediately hopped on chairs and screamed, watching the mouse flop around in the trap.

My memory of this story ends here. I probably continued screaming with my eyes closed. I don't know if my sister, Mom, or perhaps even my younger brothers scooped the trap into the dustpan and launched it outside the back door. I only remember the noise of the incident – our screams and the snap – and my approximate size relative to the chair I was standing on.

One winter evening, when I was around the same size, a larger animal disrupted the house while Mom was out in the barn milking. The faint smell of a skunk grew so intense and so quickly that I was absolutely positive the animal was in the house spraying. Panicked, I got winter coats on my sister and brothers and hustled them out the back door, around the corner of the house, and twenty yards across the snowy barnyard. I remember the warm lights glowing through the barn window high at the peak of the building. I popped open the upper and lower barn doors, and the warmth of the cows washed over us.

Ahhh, safety. Surprising Mom with bundled-up kids, I explained about the skunk in the house. Mom's incredulous look spoke to me before her voice. The strong smell had taken my imagination to a place of undeniable realism. While I was standing in the barn, it dawned on me that there had never been a skunk in the house before this, that it was impossible for a skunk to get into the house, and that I had just taken my sister and brothers ever so close to the skunk's true path by herding them outside to the barn. A skunk must have sprayed near the back door, and then the odor had slipped in through the cracks around the door, making it smell like a skunk had gotten into the house.

Similar events have taken place in our current house with Bill and me. I take care of the mice; they are still cute creatures to Bill. Getting his American citizenship didn't change his feelings toward them nor any other pesky animal.

However, the one time Bill and I both thought there was a skunk inside the house, I took the kids upstairs to our bedrooms and sent Bill in search of skunks in the basement. On second thought, it might have just been me who was convinced there was a skunk in the basement, convinced that our basement door must have been left open. Yeah, pretty sure that was just me.

Yet, my hero Bill took the helm and went scouting for imaginary skunks that evening.

# Slugs and Worms

On one wet fall trip to England, I lay in bed mouthing, "I must sleep." And my jet-lagged mind was nowhere near contemplating this possibility. That was the backdrop for a philosophical chat about slugs with then eight-year-old Liam.

In the dark at 2 a.m. English time, the last big question he posed was, "Are slugs nocturnal?" The question might have been about cows in Iowa or the squirrels at home in Massachusetts. But in England, it was slugs.

Honestly, I didn't know, but it was a thought-provoking question. As Liam drifted off, my mind latched onto the question. I think slugs just move as they can where they can. Certainly they can't think, *Ahhh, dusk is approaching! I must hurry to shelter!* No, they must just sleep where they get tired, be it day or night.

We gave up trying to get our sons adjusted to English time; they slept late every morning and went to bed no earlier than midnight each night. All day, every day, they made their way between their grandma's house and their auntie's house, which were next door to each other. The back doors were separated by wet paved patios. A week after the first slug question, I entertained yet another slug discussion in the wee English morning hours.

"Mom," Liam started hotly, "slugs are nocturnal! I stepped on one tonight walking back to Grandma's from Auntie's! My socks got all sluggy!"

I nearly gagged. English slugs are big. For a comparison, my sister-in-law held her pinky finger alongside one on the ground: it was as wide and long as her finger. Oooo-gah! I really felt for the kid! That was not worm squishing. That was creature squishing. With only socks on. I had forgotten our conversation the following morning; otherwise, I would have thrown that pair of socks away along with the ones caked in mud from a walk in the fields.

I was left wondering how big a spider, worm, bug, or rodent needs to be to elevate it to an unsquishable creature. Of course, there is no generic answer for that, for we all have different tolerance levels — as demonstrated by the mouse and my dad's boot.

The slug conversation reminded me of my small tomato patch at the house where Bill and I first lived, in Rockford, Illinois. The tomatoes thrived in the hot summer sun. They stretched up past my elbows and were loaded with blossoms and big leaves. I watered the plants nightly. It was with watering can in hand one evening that I noticed a whole stem stripped of leaves and blossoms. And another stem below that. And another. Several plants had bare green stems where, the day before, there had been a healthy tomato plant. It wasn't until I put my nose into the plant for a closer look that I saw the problem: tomato hornworms.

Having fed overnight on my tomato plants, these worms were already the size of that English slug. The hornworms had magnificent camouflage ability, being the exact same color as the tomato plant and gripping tightly to the stem that supported their weight as they ate their way along the plant. Their caterpillar body lacked fuzz and looked like leathery segmented skin with a little white dot on each segment. A harmless-to-humans black horn stuck up off their rear ends.

I ran for gloves and a pie tin, the only container I could quickly put my hands on in the garage. Then I pulled each worm off my plants and dropped it onto the tin. The dozen worms I found scuffled around in the slippery aluminum tin. I could hear their teeth tapping on the metal. If their size didn't pose enough of a challenge in how to dispose of them, the clicking of their teeth made the thought of conventional bug-squishing impossible. So says the woman who plucked headless chickens as a child. Mind you, I never actually butchered the chickens.

Writing this gives me goose bumps. I couldn't squish those hornworms. They were too far to the right on the creature spectrum. I transferred them into a Mason jar, screwed the lid on, and threw it into the garbage. If faced with this dilemma again, I will keep in mind the *Old Farmer's Almanac* suggestion of dropping them into hot soapy water. Or feeding them to your chickens. That kind of makes me want to buy some baby chicks.

# Spiders

A wolf spider sat quietly just inside Mom's back door in an old margarine bowl. Motionless. But he was only playing possum. He moved when I picked up the bowl and gently set it on the cement bench outside the back door. It reminded me of a brief spider encounter I had in England a few years ago.

Again and again, Bill's family talks about the "Hertfordshire Horror" – a large spider found in the county of Hertfordshire, England. I've heard they can be as big as the palm of your hand. Finding one in your house? The dread of that puts *Horror* in its nickname. However, with no screens and the windows flung open to catch a breeze, the invitation is extended for the Horrors and their smaller cousins to gravitate inward.

One summer night when we'd arrived in England, Bill's mum, June, announced from upstairs, "There's a spider in the bathroom!" That set the next fifteen-minute scene into action as my husband and sister-in-law, Anne, went into English spider-removal mode.

Fortunately, it was a smaller spider, not a Horror. "Stay here, Anne. I'll take care of it!" I imagined an anti-spider cape springing from Bill's shoulders as he ascended the stairs. "OK, it's under a glass. Now we need something to slide under the glass. A lid." I simply stood back and watched.

Anne came up to help, bringing some kind of a lid with her. Then came the logistical challenge of how to get the lid under the glass without the spider escaping. With a loud combined effort, the three eventually worked it out. Anne zoomed down the stairs. "OK, Bill, I've got the door open!" Bill flew out of the bathroom and down the stairs. They both went out the door and disappeared.

I stepped outside to see where they went: two blocks down the street, they released the spider. Probably after spinning in a circle three times to confuse it so it wouldn't make its way back to the house. Reminiscent of two teenagers, they walked back giggling with relief. I greeted them at the door. "You make life so difficult!" I was amazed that getting rid of a spider could take that long.

The next day, I saw a spider – not a Horror – on the ceiling in June's kitchen. It was tightly tucked into the back corner. I couldn't get it without moving the table and chairs. As the week went on, it gradually journeyed closer to the back door. On day seven and in the house by myself, I was able to reach it by standing on a kitchen chair. Squish, wipe, flush. Five seconds, job done.

I know spiders are good. They eat other bugs. But there are hundreds of thousands of them out there. This transpired secretly on English soil. Writing about it feels like a confession of guilt. I assume that I broke an English spider-protection law.

# Red-Winged Blackbirds, Gravel Dust, Feral Cats, and Pig Shit

Over spring break in Iowa a few years ago, I pulled into a parking lot and rolled my window down while waiting to meet a friend. I heard familiar birds cackling from a small grove of evergreen trees. The sound pulled my upper lip into a snarl.

Red-winged blackbirds – they nested in the ditches near Mom and Dad's house when I was growing up. In the spring, they would dive-bomb us kids when we rode our bikes on the gravel road. I was sure that "the Birds" in Alfred Hitchcock's movie must have been red-winged blackbirds. Their call reminded me that there are some things I do not miss about Iowa. I made a note to remember more of those things on this trip.

No matter the season, if you live on a gravel road, your vehicle is covered in dust. You have dust lines on the back of your jeans at calf level and probably the front of your waist – from bumping legs on the car getting into it and from leaning against the trunk to put items inside it. Limestone quarries grind this common Iowa mineral down to spread on gravel roads. The stone is soft and breaks easily when vehicles drive over it, resulting in unending dust balls spun up by tires. Dust lines on clothes are telltale signs that you live on a gravel road.

Will and his cousin played "Here Comes the Bride" at Mom and Dad's 50th vow renewal ceremony. Getting ready to head to the church, Will loaded his trumpet into the back of our rental car and leaned right up against the dirty metal. Fortunately, it was a dry day, so a few brushes with my hand knocked off the dust from his bright red polo shirt. A few days earlier after a heavy rain, I'd thought the dust on the car would get washed away – that's what happens at our house in the Northeast. However, limestone dust becomes clay-like when it gets wet. Then the sun comes out and bakes it onto the cars. A few trips down the road and the car becomes so encrusted that only a power washer can remove the build-up.

On this same trip, Liam was set on taming a feral cat at Grandpa and Grandma's, but the cats are all full-grown and wild. Liam, Will, and their cousins had been able to tame a kitten when we visited in June a couple of years earlier. It was the runt of a feral litter and starving. The kids nursed it back to health with food and were able to pet him as they fed him. They domesticated him. Skippy went on to live as a pet at my sister's house.

Normally, there are two to eight wild cats on the farm. Their eyes are shifty. The cats creep up to humans because they want food. They prance around and wind between Mom and Dad's feet, creating tripping hazards until fed or yelled at. Any sudden movement, like bending to pet them, sends them scattering. The cats navigate between farms and may disappear for a few hours or days before returning to scavenge on table scraps. Liam sees them only as cats with cuddle potential. I see them as wild animals, never to be tamed, and a threat to Mom and Dad's safety whenever they walk out their back door.

One of the best parts of the day on the farm is early morning. The sunrise on a wide horizon trickles in through the bathroom blinds and pours in through the living room windows when the curtains are pulled aside. One morning, the glow was dazzling. To get a full, unobstructed view, I slipped sandals on and opened the back door. I caught a left hook from the smell of pig shit. It knocked my vision of the sunrise right off the horizon.

Pigs are big business in Iowa. It used to be that if the wind was out of the south, the smell was bad. Now with more pig farmers on all sides of Mom and Dad's farm, it's always lingering in the air, more pungent on some days than others. That morning, I closed the door on it and went back to the living room window. I was reminded of the numerous times I'd heard that the smell of manure is the smell of money. It's much more pleasant when that smell is your own money.

There you have it: Iowa's dive-bombing red-winged blackbirds, gravel dust baked to clay on cars, freaky feral cats, and the stench of pig shit.

# The Farmer in the Family

———◆◆◆———

A couple years ago I had minor surgery, and as it was late in the day, I ended up staying overnight in the hospital. Bill came to get me in the morning. With the general anesthesia still clouding my brain, this was the first story I heard from Bill that morning.

He woke up at 5 a.m. and discovered a tarantula on the wall in our bathroom. He saw it twice, at 5 a.m. and a bit later when he woke up again. Both times it was tucked into a tight corner, and he couldn't get it with a flyswatter or capture it with a glass, so he pulled the bathroom door shut.

Actually, it was a bee that had bumbled its way into our house. I told Bill I would take care of it when I got home.

"No, I can do it," he insisted.

This happens every year. The first year we lived in Massachusetts, after finding three or four bumblebees upstairs, I had a pest control guy come out. He assured us that the bees we found were simply hitchhikers that had hopped a ride on someone's clothing. I didn't buy it for a minute.

Here is what happened: With the plunging cold temperatures gone, our rhododendron was in full bloom that spring. The ten-foot-high rhododendron grows below a second-floor bedroom window, nestled outside the portion of our house that was built in 1880.

Big bumblebees love these blossoms. They roll in the blossoms like pigs in shit.

I'm convinced that in a pollen-drunken state, they meander into a little hole in the old wooden window frame upstairs and get dazed and confused in the thin walls. Of all that enter, perhaps four a season end up inside the house. Then, far away from that sweet nectar and after the treacherous journey to the inside, the biggest one will meet a tall Englishman in a bathroom at 5 a.m.

When I got home from the hospital, I walked upstairs and right by the bumblebee. With only a little discussion between us, the kind Englishman and the squish-'em Iowan, we got rid of the bee with a flyswatter. At the top of the stairs, the bathroom door was still shut tight with no apparent crack from which the bee could have escaped. Yet, to make sure there wasn't a bee still in the bathroom, Bill slowly approached the door armed with the flyswatter in ready position. As he touched the doorknob, I stung him in the back with my finger. Oh my goodness, the poor Englishman hit the ceiling! There was no bee in the bathroom.

A couple mornings later in our barn loft, we were experiencing squirrel hell. I had fully anticipated writing "The Squirrel Saga," but oftentimes I can't write until the trauma subsides a bit, and we had been at that game for weeks. We had live squirrel traps on the roof of the barn and upstairs in the barn loft. They needed to be checked daily. We could see the one on the roof, but every day, we needed to go up to the loft

— into the corner farthest from the stairs – and check the other trap.

Here's the deal that Bill came up with: "One of my colleagues at work had a bat in her bedroom. As she put it, there are girl jobs and there are boy jobs. And the bat was a boy job. As I see it, going up to the loft to check that squirrel trap is neither a boy job nor a girl job. It's a farmer's job."

The response crossed over my lips as Grandma Mills would've concisely put it, with a sharp sting in her words:

Damn it.

# Corn's On!

On the eve of Dad's 70$^{th}$ birthday, a humid August evening, Will, Liam, and I were in Iowa helping Dad pick sweet corn. We would be "doing corn" the next day, on Dad's birthday. In the corn patch, which was probably a hundred yards long and twenty rows deep, Dad picked corn and filled five-gallon buckets while I carried full buckets to the little Chevy S-10 pickup and emptied them into the truck bed. The cornstalks shot way over our heads and were thick enough to hide Dad among them. Following their grandpa's voice, Will and Liam took the buckets back into the patch to be refilled.

The boys and I exaggerated the steps we took over the electric fence that lined the perimeter of the corn patch. It was about six inches above the ground and stopped the raccoons from entering the patch. If a few raccoons had a midnight feast and then invited their friends to come the next night and the next, a good chunk of corn would have been stripped from the stalks in a matter of a couple days.

Shortly, this conversation between Farm Dad and City Girl ensued:

"How many buckets have you emptied?" Dad asked.

"Oh, I don't know, maybe eight or twelve," I guessed.

"Haven't you been counting?" he asked.

Then it dawned on me; I should've been counting. "No."

"You haven't been counting?"

"You didn't tell me to count."

"We always count so Mom has enough for a hundred pints."

"Well, I haven't done this in fifteen years. I guess I needed a reminder to count!"

"Why, Linda Kay . . . I can't believe you didn't count." His tone was good-natured.

At dusk, we had more than enough for a hundred pints. We had a truckload. The truck full of corn sat in the drive overnight, and early the next 70th-birthday morning, Dad and I started husking corn, and the boys joined us. We pulled the layers of husk off and most of the silk, too.

Amateur corn picker that I had become, I dumped corn haphazardly into the truck bed, covering it entirely. Realizing I had goofed up the shucking system a bit, I climbed into the truck bed and pushed all the unshucked corn toward the tailgate where we could reach it. That created a designated space for us to toss the corn husks and silks into toward the front of the bed.

"I bet I'm the only one in my school who has done this!" then-nine-year-old Will said as we filled the coolers with corn.

Four big chest coolers of corn on the cob equal a hundred pints of corn kernels for the freezer. Once we had lined up the full coolers in the dining room, Dad's job ended and Mom took over. Mom and I lined the kitchen table and floor with newspaper and set up a desilking station on one end of the table and an area to cut the corn off the cob at the other end.

Maureen, Mom's friend since high school, arrived with her grandson, and the setting was complete: It was time to do corn. The three boys used dish towels to brush off the corn silks so Maureen, Mom, and I could strip kernels off the cobs.

The magic soon wore off the desilking process. The boys took breaks when there was nowhere to pile the silk-free corn and then dutifully came back when space opened up on the table. They were such troupers. The desilking was tough going at times, but they finished.

I had seen those piles through the eyes of a seven- and nine-year-old. I remember vegetables and fruit that needed to be cleaned, stemmed, broken, or cut up. The amounts were monstrous. Here, much like walking beans, was the true grit of farming. Of growing and freezing our own food. Of sticking to a task until it was finished.

Mom's job shifted once we had big pans of kernels. They needed to be blanched for three minutes, spread out to cool in front of the fan, and then loaded into pint-size freezer bags that were labeled with the year.

Maureen and I kept cutting as Mom followed the circuit of those final processing tasks. Aunt Alison arrived later in the afternoon. "I heard you were doing corn. I thought I would come up and help." Aunt Alison stepped into the blanching–cooling–bagging circuit with Mom.

Toward the end of the afternoon, Liam walked through the kitchen. "BLAH! YUCK! What did I step in???"

Ah yes, that feeling of sweet, sticky corn milk on the bottom of your foot and of dragging newspaper along with you as you try to walk away.

"Mom, there just aren't many kids who have done this, right?" Will asked. "We picked it, husked it, cleaned it, and bagged it! We did it all from beginning to end!"

Yes, from beginning to end.

# Tolerance of Cow Manure between Your Toes

There are forty-eight years of stories that could be written about the barn on Mom and Dad's farm in northeast Iowa where I grew up. Now, raising teenage sons in the city, I have stories bubbling in my head with a common theme: tolerance. Of fresh cow manure between your toes. Of picking up eggs from underneath a mean setting hen. Of keeping two paces ahead of a nasty spurred rooster.

On a visit home for Christmas in 2014, I had a flashback to a winter when I was around ten years old, about the same age as my sons were on this trip. The setting was three feet from the barn, specifically at the water hydrant used to fill the cattle's water tank. A metal watering pipe with a little basin at one end, shaped like Grandpa Mills's tobacco pipe, was hooked with a heavy #9 wire over the hydrant spout, and the long metal tube ran through the gate to the water tank. To fill the tank, we lifted up the hydrant handle and let an ice-cold river flow through the pipe into the tank. In the winter, Dad used straw bales to insulate the base of the hydrant to keep it from freezing. However, if the temperature stayed below freezing long enough, the insulation could fail. Back then there was no water heater in the tank, nor was water pumped into the tank automatically. We filled it manually. If water froze in the base of the hydrant, it needed to be thawed so the cattle could get water.

That's what we were doing one particularly cold day. I stood on the south side of the hydrant facing the barn. Dad stood on the north side of the hydrant with his back to the barn. In the late afternoon light, he used a blowtorch to thaw the pipe. The sun was sinking, the temperature was too cold, and the wind chill was spectacular. My feet were locked in place as I helped Dad.

However, I have absolutely no recollection of *how* I helped him. After the sun sank, perhaps I held a flashlight. The memory is so visceral, I want a winter coat to protect me from that crazy cold. We were out there for well over an hour, me standing, watching; Dad silently, stoically working. I can't imagine I was much help. The cold ate at me as I hoped Dad would give up and call it a night. He didn't. I remember thinking, *I'm not helping at all. Why can't I go in the house?* But I couldn't move. My feet stood firm next to my dad. How could I walk away and leave him out there by himself?

In early March 2015, an opportunity for practicing tolerance arose back in Massachusetts. After a loud squabble in the back of the van on the drive home from school, I parked the car and announced that I would be confiscating all electronics for the rest of the day. Why? Because that's what I used to do when my fuse went: I took away the thing that gave the most instantaneous joy. I admit, and my whole family knows, that this move never effected change the way I had hoped it would. Nevertheless, I kept doing it for many years.

I parked the van and sent my older son, Will, into the house to do his homework. I took Liam out to the deck with me to take down dead evergreen boughs from Christmas that were wired to the railings of the deck and hanging around the front door. We needed to unwrap ten or more long strings of white lights from forty feet of boughs.

Our twinkle lights had looked awesome in our record hundred inches of snow that winter. I'd spent a whole afternoon putting them up. Now, the transformation away from winter was more laborious. I gave Liam a prickly bough to unwrap.

"How do I do this?!?" *Start at one end.* "I'm never going to finish this!" *Keep going.* "OK, I'm done." *No you are not. We'll work on this one together.* "Look, now we're done!" *No we're not. Now we move to the front yard.* "More?" *Yes.*

The boughs around the front door came down much more easily. As I freed each set of lights, I directed Liam to put it on the deck at the back of the house. With only two sets left to untangle, Liam said, "Am I done now? Can I go in?" *No; hold this string of lights.* The bundle of lights didn't need to be held, but I needed his feet held to the ground to see the end of this project. Liam held it, not knowing why.

Scraps of needles scattered all over the steps. I swept with a big barn broom and told Liam to pick up the little clusters of needles on the ground. I watched as he scuffed them into the snow with his boot. "Whatever you don't pick up now, you will be picking up after the snow melts." He uncovered them and picked them up. I pulled the dead evergreen wreath off the door.

We put away the wire cutters, broom, lights, boughs, and wreath. "OK, I'm done!" *No, not yet.* Wisps of steam escaped from his ears.

In the garage, I found the spring wreath and asked Liam to hang it on the front door. I told him it was a crown, and he put it on his head. "OK," I said, "turn it any way you like and hang it on the nail."

He followed my instructions.

"Now, every time we come home and you see our front door, that wreath will remind you how much you helped today."

That spring, Liam noticed the wreath daily.

# Headlights on a Hot, Humid Gravel Road

Thirty-two years separated two summer evenings when Dad was out looking for me after dark. The stifling humidity of summer often reminds me of those evenings and the sight of those familiar headlights coming down the gravel road.

The first time was when I was a senior in high school and late getting home one evening. I had said I would be home by ten o'clock. I wasn't getting into trouble. I had just run into a friend, started to chat, and lost track of time. Around eleven o'clock on the gravel road leading to our house, I recognized the headlights. And Dad recognized mine.

Living in the country, we had only five or six neighbors within a mile radius, so we recognized cars and trucks day and night. The height of the headlights on Dad's four-wheel-drive truck, together with the fact that I was meeting a car at this time of night on the deserted road a half mile from our house, left no doubt in my mind who was driving. I'm sure similar clues led Dad to slow down as he approached me driving our family's four-door Oldsmobile.

Side by side, we both rolled down our windows. The humidity smacked my face as the dust rolled into my eyes.

"Get home." That's all he said. Remembering that evening still sends waves of guilt through me.

The second time, I was 45 and had my two sons with me visiting Iowa during a hot, humid summer. We'd been in town picking up a few groceries and visiting my brother and his family. When we left, I told my brother we were heading to Mom and Dad's.

When I left my brother's house, the temperature was brutal and the air thick with humidity. I took a slight detour and picked up a gallon of ice cream at the grocery store for our Amish neighbors. I thought they might enjoy a cool treat the next day. As I drove down the highway, lightning bugs flashed but moved so slowly, it seemed they were treading water. After ten minutes, I made a left-hand turn from asphalt onto the gravel road to get to Mom and Dad's. It was just nearly dark when I drove past our neighbors' house. I saw ten shadows gathered outside around picnic tables. The three-generation extended family was still up and sitting outside, begging for a slight breeze. I braked, reversed, and pulled into their driveway. My friend Clara saw it was me and immediately walked over to the car.

"I thought you might like some ice cream. I was going to bring it over tomorrow, but since you're still up . . ."

"Oh my gosh, thank you so much!"

The word *ice cream* put a cool energy into everyone. One of the kids disappeared into the house and came back with ten spoons, and the family passed around the gallon of vanilla ice cream.

The boys and I plopped on a picnic bench to visit. We'd just stopped at the Dairy Queen in town, so we didn't need another helping of ice cream. My son, four-year-old Liam, silently studied everyone, then pointed at Clara's bearded brother-in-law, Ben. "Hey, are you from *Little House on the Prairie?*"

Fortunately it was dark by then so no one could see my cheeks burning red. Ben wore a long beard plus suspenders and a work shirt. "Yes," I said, "Ben does look a little like Pa from *Little House on the Prairie*, doesn't he? But he's not. Clara and her family are Amish, and they dress differently than we do."

As I was explaining, Ben interjected, "Oh, do you read those books? We love them!" As it happened, we had been reading Laura Ingalls Wilder books, watching the TV show – and making homemade butter.

Liam and Will went off with the younger kids to look at the two-month-old kittens. A few minutes later, Liam came back to show one to me. He had a firm grasp of it. Around its neck. I jumped up to rescue the kitten. "Sorry, he's never held a kitten before!" I explained. My comment drew a few puzzled looks. Knowing how to hold a kitten comes easily when you are four years old and live on a farm where spring brings babies of all kinds: calves, piglets, chicks, and kittens.

"Really?" said Ben. "Come here, Liam. Let me show you how to hold a kitten." In seconds, Liam was cradling his first kitten in the crook nook of his arm, petting it with his other hand.

With full darkness settling in, we said good night. We cranked the AC in the car and headed down the road. A hundred yards from Clara's driveway, there were those headlights. I was seventeen again. We met. We rolled down the windows.

"Where have you been?"

"At Clara's."

"We have been trying to call you!"

"Oh. . . . My cell phone was in the car. I didn't hear it ring. I'm so sorry, Dad."

One of my favorite spots was − and still is − sitting with friends and visiting, without a cell phone.

# Union Station

"How did your crops do this year?"

Stunned, my dad thought this thirty-something woman, a stranger at the small Cedar Rapids, Iowa, airport was pretty intuitive to walk up to him and ask this question.

"I guess she recognizes a farmer when she sees one!" Dad said.

This woman was an Illinois native who now lives in DC. She, too, was a farmer's daughter. Her father probably looked much the same as mine.

I wonder what she noticed first. Clean work boots and pinstriped bib overalls? The sleek black jacket with the small Pioneer seed corn symbol stitched on the left chest? The black Garst seed corn cap? Or the plain black mock turtleneck under the bibs?

All in all, Dad was one spiffed-up farmer with these black dress clothes blending seamlessly with his new blue-and-white-striped bib overalls and work boots. Dad looked sharp. He could have been going to a farm convention in those clothes. Dad was heading east with me to spend two weeks with my family. He had finished picking corn and beans and was ready for a little getaway.

That morning started early for me in Indianapolis. After a three-day conference there, I was up at 4:30 a.m. so I could catch a plane to Chicago and then another to Cedar Rapids, Iowa, where Dad was going to meet me at the airport. His day started the night before. Anticipating the trip, he didn't sleep.

Late morning, I deplaned in Cedar Rapids and said hello to the other farmer's daughter. Then Dad and I got on the road in his little Chevy S10 pickup truck heading to Chicago: a four-hour drive ahead of us. We were going to catch a 9:30 p.m. train out of Union Station that would take us to Boston – a twenty-four-hour journey on the rails.

After getting lost and driving in circles trying to find a Cracker Barrel restaurant in Davenport, Iowa, a Mississippi River city, I easily made my way to a parking spot at one of O'Hare Airport's remote lots. Driving the Midwest grids between Iowa and Illinois and recognizing north and south four-lanes around O'Hare felt like putting on a familiar glove. I don't have a glove like that in Boston. Yet.

"Now what?" asked Dad as we parked the truck.

We followed the crowd and moved our bags and suitcases to a bus-stop shelter. I looked at three people and explained that we needed to catch a taxi to Union Station. One man, on his way to Singapore, gave us directions. "So," he said, looking at Dad, "you're going to Boston. How do you feel about seafood?"

Dad replied evenly, "I love a good burger."

Laughing out loud, our guide replied, "Now, *that's* an Iowa farmer!" He herded us aboard the shuttle bus, then onto a connecting tram. The first tram stop was the international terminal, where we could catch at taxi.

From the tram platform, I looked around for an elevator.

"What are you carrying *that* for?" asked an airport employee. *That* was Dad's big suitcase without wheels; I was unsure if the employee had ever seen one this size before. "Wait here. I'll find a cart." When he came back, I thanked him as he directed us to the elevator that would take us to the lower level where taxis waited.

The elevator doors opened, and the international terminal felt familiar. I dove into the crowd, glancing behind me to be sure that Dad stayed on my heels. How many times had my husband, Bill, and I returned from visiting his family in England right through those gates? The terminal bustled, activity driven by chaos. Yet in the middle of all that, three men stood facing west, quietly murmuring prayers. I was reminded that walking on the right is part of our American culture. People moved in the direction they needed to go.

"Are we close to the door?" Dad asked, just loudly enough that I could hear him over my shoulder.

"Stay close to me," I replied.

After maneuvering through the airport, we landed in a taxi. From the back seat, Dad asked, "How long have you been driving?"

The upbeat taxi driver replied in an accented voice, "It will take about 30 minutes with Sunday evening traffic." He thought Dad had asked how long the drive to Union Station would be.

I said, "How long have you driven a taxi?"

"Ohhh, about five years."

"Where are you from?" I asked.

"Nepal, where Mt. Everest is. I've been here about eight years. I love Chicago!"

Then it dawned on me. Dad was asking about the cabbie's ability to drive, a kind of pretest to help him judge how tightly he would need to hold on. I was asking about the driver, his culture, his life.

"There you go. Finally here!" announced the driver after a very smooth ride free of any aggressive maneuvers or heavy braking.

With four hours to wait, we walked into Union Station and found a table. I felt electric. After all, the only place I had gotten us lost was in Davenport, Iowa. My part was done. Now we relied on the train for the rest of the journey.

Dad looked ashen.

"I just realized how very strange all this must be to you, Dad."

He nodded as he ate his Chicago hot dog.

After that bite to eat and reading a few newspapers, Dad and I zigzagged down an escalator and through a crowded hallway to our boarding lounge. I led the way with an occasional glance to make sure Dad was still with me. I turned the last corner and looked behind me, and he wasn't there. A silly jab of panic, as if I had lost my two-year-old, swept over me. I backtracked twenty yards to find him perched against a wall with that Iowan tight-lipped, tough, stoic look awash on his face.

The look I see in my bathroom mirror every morning before I take a shower.

Dad thought I was checking things out, and he didn't want to get wound up in the coil of people who were waiting for another train. I coaxed him to follow me again. With over an hour before we could board the Amtrak train to Boston, we garnered two seats in the nearly empty lounge.

Eight small children were taking advantage of the wide-open space before the twenty-four-hour train ride. Three moms, no dads, sat waiting. Dreading? The tolerance for what behavior was okay was uncertain among the moms at first. Then one mom loudly pulled aside the oldest boy, probably around seven years old, for some antic. "Go look at that wall! *And don't look at me!*"

A bit later, a train station employee brought back a three-year-old little girl from down the hall who had wandered out of her mom's sight, saying something to the effect that it wasn't safe, for other passengers or the little girl.

Four well-dressed 60- to 70-ish-year-old women came in chatting loudly. From their bewildered looks, they weren't sure if they were in the right lounge. The briskness of their language and accent made me think that they were probably from Eastern Europe.

A family of Mennonites – mom, dad, and three teenage girls – sat in a corner of the lounge. The calico dresses, pinafores, and squared, starched white bonnets identified them as Mennonites, not Amish. The Amish women who live near Mom and Dad in Iowa wear solid colors and softer, non-angular white bonnets.

A young white woman with a ukulele sticking out of her backpack sat on the floor, casually drinking a can of beer. A young black man with dreads, a quiet voice, and an unidentified accent approached her and her ukulele. Within seconds of the ukulele coming out, she was leading a mini–music session with eight kids clustered around her, each wanting a turn with this exotic instrument. They argued over turns.

"Just make sure everyone gets a turn. Play a little bit, then pass it around. *Share*." Her voice was soft and idealistic. Had this modern-day young hippie seen three of the boys practice punching one another per Mom's direction? These boys practiced survival more than they did sharing, yet the ukulele jerkily made its way around the circle of kids.

On his own, a middle-aged Amish man, looking more conservative than the Mennonite father, entered the lounge. A very obese man came into the lounge and sat down. People cleared around him. His clothing didn't cover his stomach, and the body odor would surely get worse during a twenty-four-hour train ride.

The rest of the cast filtered in quietly, nearly unnoticed. Many carried pillows and blankets. Couples of all ages. Young men traveling together. Some pierced and tattooed, and some not. Young women traveling together. All looking at their personal devices more than at one another. Older women traveling in pairs, already looking tired.

Just before the boarding call, three young nuns in full habit whooshed into the lounge. Their round, plain faces were framed by a layer of tight, white, starched material, with loose black fabric flowing over the strict white. I smiled and felt that with their presence, we had all been blessed.

This tiny microcosm of humanity, including a farmer and his daughter, crowded the boarding gate facing that one thing we all had in common at this moment: a long train ride east out of Union Station.

# Interlude

---

"A good snapshot stops a moment
from running away."

Eudora Welty

# Dichotomy of Place

Some fifty years after being born in a small town in Iowa, I live in what's considered, by Massachusetts standards, to be a small town north of Boston. Our farm in Iowa was eight miles from the town where I went to elementary and high school. My hometown in Iowa had a population of around 2,000. My hometown in the Northeast has a population of over 27,000.

When I fly over soybean fields and cornfields near the Cedar Rapids, Iowa, airport, I feel like I'm truly coming home as I look down at the patchwork quilt of green in the summer, gold in the fall, and black dirt before the snow falls in the winter or after it melts in the spring. The patches of fields are outlined by dark fence rows and scattered trees. Landing there in the winter, I see red barns punctuating the snowy landscape.

Flying into the Cedar Rapids airport gives me the same feeling as did returning home from college in October of my freshman year to attend my high school's homecoming football game. Under bright lights, hearing the announcer, watching the marching band – there was something comforting in revisiting that known place when my future was so geared toward newness. College meant new people, new places, new thinking, new studying. New, new, new. The old was soothing.

Flying into Logan International Airport, I also get a feeling of coming home. As the Harbor Islands and Boston skyline come into view, I know I'm close to our house, to our family's life. However, on the final approach, even after thirteen years of flying into Logan, I turn my head away from the window. Logan's runway juts out into the Boston Harbor, and planes linger just above the water – and appear to be landing in the harbor – before a paved strip miraculously appears just moments before the wheels touch down. This unsettled anxiousness before landing reminds me that this isn't my first home, that landing on a patchwork quilt is easier than this hovering over whitecapped water. While a sentiment of homecoming wraps around me when landing in the Midwest amongst the cornfields, that prickly landing over the Atlantic reminds me that I'm a long way from my original Midwest home.

In February 2019, I flew home at short notice when my mom was sick and was admitted to the local hospital. Since there was a mixed precipitation forecast in the Midwest, I flew into Chicago, then drove to Iowa to avoid weather delays at the small Cedar Rapids airport. I slept at Mom and Dad's house and woke up early each morning to get to the hospital before the doctor did his 7 a.m. rounds.

This happened to be the week when the temperature in Iowa dropped to an all-time low, creating wind chills of fifty-five degrees below zero. Daily there was a wintry mix falling from the afternoon sky, yet most mornings I woke up to infinitely wide horizon sunrises — and on one spectacularly cold morning, a spectacular double sunrise. Created by ice crystals falling through the sun's rays at just the right angle, that morning's powerful sundog left me wondering which bright ball of light was the true sun. Seven days later, Mom was out of the hospital and on the mend, and I drove four hours back to Chicago the night before I flew home. As the jet ascended out of O'Hare the next morning, I saw the hot pink ball breaking through a cloud on the horizon of Lake Michigan, the Chicago skyline sleepily nestled in the foreground. With a strong tailwind, that flight out of O'Hare was the shortest ever back to Boston, an hour and forty minutes.

Unlike my normal landings at Boston's Logan Airport when I avert my eyes from the view, this time I glued my eyes to the window, forcing myself to watch and to hold confidence in the pilot as we glided what looked like only a few feet over the water. I held tight, convincing myself that a smooth landing strip would soon appear and catch the jet's tires.

The abruptness of this change in location — from calling one place "home" and then having less than a two-hour flight out of the Midwest to "home" 1,600 miles away — left me reeling a bit. The journey that I had made so many times struck me differently on that return trip to Boston. I couldn't find firm footing in this dichotomy of place.

As I see it, where a person leaves footprints on this earth gives direction to all else, and at a most basic level to food, clothing, and shelter. Place anchors the building of culture. The culmination of intellectual, artistic, and religious traits further envelops and defines a people. But where a person's foot touches the earth, that place called home . . . it's solid ground. Not an opinion or an idea, but solid ground.

At the Museum of Science in Boston, there is a large wall of screens depicting caricature fish in an ocean. From the *Star Trek*–like control stations in front of the screens, kids – and at least one adult – control the characteristics and creation of each fish, including the direction that they swim and their schooling behaviors. If an enemy approaches a school, a push of a button scatters the fish. The outer edge of that divergence, of a whole shattered into parts, is where I am in describing this place called New England. "Codfish" is like watching a fireworks display in reverse. I'm chasing pieces, trying to harness and articulate them into "place."

This is in direct opposition to reflections and writings in "Cornfields." The Midwest is a place where my feet dropped onto black soil every morning for nearly forty years. Where cornstalks' roots ground themselves firmly two to six feet into that dirt, as deep as necessary to find water, until the spring when the fields are chisel plowed and what's remaining of the old roots are gently broken up, opening the soil for the new season's crop. There is no frenzied scattering of cornstalks. Those roots lock deep into the earth.

When I drove from Iowa to Massachusetts in April 2005, I crossed the New York/Massachusetts border and wondered how on earth people made a living here amongst all the trees. No open farm fields on this route, only the Berkshire Hills covered in trees. And those hills gave way to cities, growing more compact the closer I got to the Atlantic. Strangely, standing on the shores of the Atlantic that spring felt oddly familiar to me. Once again, I was at the edge of a wide-open horizon. And this ocean? *This* is an aquatic farmland.

My writing in "Cornfields" is a reflection of a solid chunk of time, an era. My writing in "Codfish" is a stream of consciousness, snapshots from a still-new place, where my feet drop close to the Atlantic Ocean rather than next to Iowa cornfields. "Codfish" is an interpretation of a place more immediate than "Cornfields." Here, I write about this new place and what rises from it – oftentimes through a Midwestern lens as we Malcolms create our own place in New England.

# Codfish

---

"The events in our lives happen in a
sequence in time, but in their significance
to ourselves they find their own order,
a timetable not necessarily — perhaps
not possibly — chronological. The time
as we know it subjectively is often the
chronology that stories and novels follow:
it is the continuous thread of revelation."

Eudora Welty

# Heat on the Annisquam

When we renovated our house in 2012, we had to move out for a good portion of the summer. We found a big old house to rent in Annisquam, Massachusetts, overlooking the tidal river of the same name. The river connected the Annisquam Harbor to the north and the Gloucester Harbor to the south. Both ends of the river lead to open waters of the Atlantic. Annisquam is a neighborhood in the town of Gloucester, located on Cape Ann. This is Massachusetts's "other cape." While Cape Cod is known for its beautiful beaches and summer retreats, this part of Cape Ann feels more like a working community. Gloucester is a no-frills fishing community on the Atlantic.

The house on the Annisquam had the shore's pulse. A lifetime of that pulse. The vinyl kitchen and dining room floors reflected the hardiness needed to live by the sea. Sand from the river's beach. Water from a lobster pot. Dirt from the crumbling paved street. All of the residue from summer days digging for clams, dining with friends, and walking uphill back from the dock. That aura sank into us through and through.

We kept the old wooden windows open wide, upstairs and down. The near ocean breeze was the only coolant in the house – a fact that nearly broke the deal for me. I'm an air conditioning worshipper on hot summer days. Light woolen blankets were on each of the ten beds. I immediately removed all of those. This was summer in the Northeast!

We ventilated sun-soaked rooms by leaving ceiling fans on every day and throughout each night. I like ceiling fans about as much as I like the heat. But they were the only choice for any comfort. The daytime air in these rooms was heavy and heated, especially in that dreaded noon-to-four portion of the days. But after that, the evenings were capable of great variety.

At the going-to-bed hours when the house held the heat, I surrendered to it. Sheets off. Fan on. Windows open. Our bedroom at the corner of the house faced the river and benefitted from a set of windows on both exterior walls. We kept the bedroom door across the hall from us open so we had a third source of airflow through that room's open windows.

All doors had big heavy conch seashells anchoring them open. At first we kicked these weights aside. It was quicker to open and close the doors that way. However, within the first couple days, we had experienced enough gunshots ricocheting through our flesh – created by slamming doors – that we fell into the habit of using the shells.

From my bed, I could see Annisquam Harbor Light. The lighthouse is on a little belly that juts out into the river, so I saw the light from about two miles away from my bedroom window, as the crow flies. On hot, thick, humid nights, I lay still on my right side and watched the light. Lying motionless was more effective than continually tossing to find a cool spot of cotton sheet. The light held my gaze, and I counted seconds between the flashes of light. Beacon. Two, three, four, five, six, seven. Beacon. I didn't lose myself counting innumerable sheep. My eyes drifted shut watching and counting that rhythm, time after time. I shared my system with Bill. At the end of summer, we were going to miss having that perpetual rotating light lull us to sleep.

By morning, the air had cooled and was pleasant. The sun woke us, and soft breezes blew away the sleep. The house was chipper in the morning. It felt like a cotton sheet that had been aired out overnight on a clothesline – that kind of freshness.

One night, Bill and I flew out of bed with bangs and cracks of a storm that had blown up in the middle of the night. Rain was blowing through the open windows; the wind whipped through the bedrooms, making the curtains flap with the intensity of a Midwestern tornado. With six bedrooms, twenty bedroom windows needed to be closed to keep the inside dry. The old wooden sash windows fought with us. Original to the house, most raged with character, but some had simply given up the fight, forgetting how the weight system worked. This resulted in an occasional slam as startling as the bedroom doors slamming shut.

One early morning while it was still dark, we woke up to a horrible stench. Something dead was outside our window. Despite the heat, we made our way around to the windows and closed them. It didn't help the indoor air much, for the odor was thoroughly inside and had the strength of a skunk spraying under an open window. It was one of those times you think the skunk *must* have gotten into the house because the scent is so strong. I envisioned a whale – or, most likely, a very large dead fish – washed up on the shore, but in fact, there were no waves on our little piece of water. It was a river. So the beast wouldn't have washed up. More aptly, it would have been left behind by the outgoing tide. By morning, the smell was gone and the tide was high. We never knew what decaying creature, or group of creatures, had created that smell of rot.

On another night, we were tucked into our hot, humid beds when a cooling breeze came through. It was gradual at first and felt comfortable; then it was downright cold. We dug out those thin woolen blankets.

The house outthought us and through natural consequences reminded us of its summer cadence – the unflinching need for conch shell doorstops and wool blankets.

# Annisquam. Fourth of July. Fireworks. Fishing.

We were in Annisquam for the Fourth of July in 2012. We ventured away from the quiet house looking for a traditional fireworks display in Gloucester. We drove around looking for a spot to avoid the loud and crazy festivities at Gloucester Harbor. We found a quiet park opposite the harbor with space for our sons to run around while we waited for the first bang. It was far enough away that the bangs, swizzles, whistles, and chasers didn't force the boys to watch with hands over their ears. We named the fireworks: gold waterfalls, pyrite rocks, spiders, and whistlers.

The following morning, we gave ourselves permission to simply sit and read, only fidgeting enough to scratch the combined fifty no-see-um bites we had from early evenings outside. No-see-ums are flying teeth – tiny, tiny bugs that you can't see or feel until they bite. The choice was to go inside or spray on a thick coating of bug spray at 6 p.m. No-see-ums are immune to the traditional Deet bug sprays. Instead we used a bug spray with a combination of natural ingredients, including lemongrass, citronella, and geranium oils. Despite being revolted by the stench of this combination, I preferred taking nightly baths to feeding flying teeth.

With threatening clouds overhead, at midday the river was quiet and the tide was in. After meeting Ed, a retired commercial fisherman, earlier that week on the beach, Liam was ready to throw in a hook. Liam hadn't flinched as he watched Ed work the hook through the eyes of an eight-inch herring that he was using as bait. Ed missed a couple good bites while chatting with us, so we didn't actually see him catch a fish from the river. We took his word for it.

The next day, we had a lesson from a very knowledgeable and patient manager of an outdoor store on rigging up a fishing pole and what bait to use. Each of us Malcolms left the store with a fishing rod. The boys cast their first lines later that same day.

Apparently, there are 28-inch striped bass — "stripers" — as well as bluefish in the Annisquam River. I fear catching a fish since I can identify only Caribbean reef fish and Iowa bullheads. According to Ed, bluefish are swimming teeth, so they should be easy to identify. Ed had shown me the needle-nosed pliers he used to remove hooks from the mouths of bluefish. Consequently, we bought a multipurpose tool: a set of needle-nose pliers/line cutters.

On the first visit to the 12 x 15-foot public dock, it was soon apparent that nothing would be hauled in. It was a casting, reeling, and untangling session. I was relieved, for taking a fish off the hook was making me squeamish just imagining it. While this practice was going on, a small boat pulled up to the dock, and we met the neighbors who lived across the street from the dock. Rich information was gathered during this brief introduction. The woman who had lived here more than fifty years knew how to clean and fillet fish. As a kid, I had watched Granddad skin and gut hundreds of bullheads but had never learned to do it myself. Bill had never fished as a kid, so he was not prepared to clean fish either.

The next day, we again went to the dock to fish. Bill and I lugged a big blue bucket with us. I also took a heavy beach towel to use as a lid, should we catch a big fish. On the walk to the dock, I checked out the shade tree where I could leave the bucket of fish as I dashed up to the neighbors' house to plead for help. All this planning was for naught. The day's outing was yet again just a practice session.

The week after the Fourth of July, we continued to throw lines into the Annisquam River. From the beach or the dock, there was a lot of ducking, casting, and reeling. Plus midair swinging of metal hooks. And plunked-down rods when the kids had to jump into the river to cool down, leaving baited hooks and one barefooted griping mother on the dock. And giggling swimmers in the water.

For the perfectionists in our house, fishing is a test of patience. Like golf, it's not a matter of simply swinging a club or casting a line and getting the ball in the hole or a fish on the hook. Both are games of variables. Of problem-solving. Of remaining calm when the perfect cast doesn't land ten yards in front of you in the middle of the river channel but twenty yards to the right of you.

Over three people and a walkway to the dock next to you. And anchors on the seaweed-covered lines holding that dock in place. The look of horror brought to the face of a perfectionist in this event was predictable.

Then, the diagnosis of the problem. First, good job not hooking any of the three people standing on the dock with you. Now gently reel in the line, following it with your rod as you go. Yank, yank, yank at the scene of the stuck bobber, weight, and hook. But we yanked in the direction that pulled the tooth on the hook even deeper into a submerged log. Looks like we need to cut the fishing line. But it's the hand-chosen, neon yellow bobber! What next? I could jump in and get it. But I don't have trunks, and the water is pretty cold. Hey, I could cut the line, wait for the tide to go out, and then get my bobber! Yes! And in the meantime, you get to learn how to string your own fishing line.

We hadn't even gotten to bait type or to depth of bait in the water, never mind the true want of catching a fish. Every seasoned fisherman and woman creates one solely designed path for a particular spot or fish species. The trick is weaving the path through trial and error, and not as the crow flies. Not as the perfectionists will it.

# The Cape Cod Beach Cottage

---

When Will was ten and Liam was eight, we caught a short early-summer vacation the first week after school was out. All I wanted was simple quiet for a few days. I found an original Cape Cod beach cottage in Yarmouth near the beach. The little cottage hadn't been touched structurally since it had been built in the 1950s. The black vinyl *46* house number on the doorframe was anchored above a painted-over *9*. While the other cottages had been built around, up, or over, ours sat a bit curmudgeonly on a corner lot. To all that fluff around it? Bah, humbug. Still house number 9.

The charmed pinewood walls were dotted with original windows. Each had one pull/push peg hold-and-lock system. Up for a breeze and down for warmth. The old painted wood floors in the two bedrooms and living room rang out with "I'm OK with sand." The vinyl floor in the kitchen was the same. It was tacked down at the doorway adjoining the living room. The sand-colored area rug in the living room was threadbare. The house was made to welcome a bit of the outdoors in. No fuss made in keeping grit from underfoot.

Weeks before the trip, I made the decision that this was going to be an electronics-free vacation. I confided in Bill. "Good luck with that," he said. He wasn't coming down to join us until the last half of the week.

I shared the plan with Will a few days before we left. After a little processing, he asserted, "OK. I can do that."

I told Liam an hour before we left. "What?!?!"

I packed the van to the gills with building blocks, craft supplies, swords and shields, and books. Drawing paper, beach gear, puzzles, and books. A magic kit, coolers of food, pantry goods, and books. Toilet paper, soap, clothes, and books.

I didn't pack computers or iPods. I didn't turn on the GPS as we left our house. The boys had maps of the Cape and written directions. Once in Yarmouth, their voices navigated me to the cottage.

That evening, we each carved out a niche, and we read. The calm soaked through us. The next morning, more of the same. Why did it feel *so* relaxing? Midweek, I figured it out. Leaving electronics at home meant there was an omission of relentless, needling questions: "When can I get on?" "It's 8 a.m.; can I play now?" "How long can I play?" "Why won't you let me play more?" "Can I play in the morning and then again in the afternoon?" This electronics-driven sublanguage wasn't spoken for a week.

At 3 a.m. the first night, I awoke feeling cold. I had shut the windows at 11 p.m., but the chill from the ocean air was still around us. Coming up from the floorboards? In through the cracks around windows and doors?

After the weeks spent on the Annisquam River two years before, I was convinced there must have been warm summer blankets tucked away somewhere. I bumbled around in the dark looking for them. In my end-to-end walk of this little cottage, I felt the years of ocean life rolling under my feet. The gentle up-and-down patter of the floorboards, an occasional dip under the vinyl in the kitchen, and an even more noticeable rise in the bathroom. The floors ebbed and flowed, reflecting the same patterns at the ocean's edge just a minute's walk away. This little cottage had felt the sea. It had ridden tandem for many years.

Not finding any blankets inside, I went barefoot through dewy grass out to my van for extra covers. My first step outside smelled like a walk into a bag of fresh clams. The cool air was bursting with ocean. I grabbed two fleece blankets from the van and tucked them over the boys. I put on a sweatshirt and went back to bed. By 10 a.m. the next day, the smell brought on by warming dampness had changed to ripe old clams baking in the sun.

Poking around that morning, I found extra blankets in a hidden closet – when the bedroom door was open, the closet door was shut. Giddy delight.

# Hillbilly Joe

The summer of 2010, the Malcolm house was fully entrenched in summer mode. While Bill was buried in the World Cup soccer games, Will and Liam were buried in dirt. A water hose and sprayer had quickly curbed "I'm bored." It was a beautiful thing – until a necessary reentry into civilization.

We needed to make a quick stop at my doctor's office. Liam was lounging in a chair on the deck, dressed only in elastic-waist khakis, sipping his cold drink. I envied my son's summer freedom, yet I had to interrupt his freshly-Liam-made lemonade sipping with "grab a shirt, a book, and your shoes."

Movement ensued. A shirt went on. In the van, I could see Liam reading a book as I pulled out of the drive. Forty-five minutes later and after three other drive-thru errands, I turned into the parking lot of the doctor's office. I glanced at Liam's feet and asked him where his shoes were.

"Do I need them?" Liam asked, glancing up from his book.

"He didn't bring a book either," Will added.

"But he's reading a book," I said.

"That's mine."

There were no shoes or socks in the van. Not a single pair of soccer or baseball cleats. The only wardrobe pieces were two bras in the back that I'd yanked off the deck railing before I drove away from the house – in case anyone stopped by the house while we were away, I didn't want them to see my hand-washables drying.

Once parked, I saw a bench in the shade outside the office building. I shooed the boys to the bench. Liam skipped over the hot pavement with a book he had found under the seat. The V-neck of his shirt was in the back.

"Hey, Hillbilly Joe, your shirt is on backwards, too!"

Hillbilly Joe smiled at the mention of his new name. Giggling, he said, "Mom, I guess I'm not very well prepared today!"

I asked for a quick appointment, explaining that I had a shoeless hillbilly son waiting outside for me. The moms in the office laughed, and I received the fastest service ever. I found the boys on the bench where I had left them. Always a welcome sight in these situations.

You'd think this boy was on his grandma and grandpa's farm in Iowa.

# Midwest Girl Goes Shopping for Codfish

Every year since we were married, Bill's family has visited us for two weeks in the summer. Normally, the summers in the Midwest and the Northeast are consistently sunnier than summer in England. So not only do we get to see one another, they also have a good hot summer holiday.

A couple of years after we moved to Massachusetts, I was doing a special grocery shop for Bill's sister, Anne. She had asked me to pick up some frozen cod that was already in a butter sauce. We had done this often when we lived in the Midwest. This would be a quick, easy meal for my nephew after their family returned from a day at Good Harbor Beach, their favorite beach on Cape Ann. The bag of frozen buttered cod could be plopped in boiling water, and dinner would be ready in minutes.

I couldn't find cod in the frozen section of my local supermarket. I approached the fish counter. "I'm looking for frozen cod. Where would I find that?"

The look and the pause from the man at the fish counter was more telling than the words "Why would you *want* that?" uttered in his Boston accent.

*Yes, why am I standing ten miles from the Atlantic wondering where to find frozen cod?*

"Well, maybe I'll just take a big fillet, cut it up, and freeze it myself."

The look. The pause. Followed by "Why would you want to do *that*?"

I gave in. I bought a packet of powdered Hollandaise sauce and a big ol' codfish fillet. For dinner that night, everyone would be having fresh cod brought in from the Atlantic that morning.

# Jingle Shells

Finding contentment with the neighborhood in Yarmouth, Cape Cod, where we rented our little beach cottage in 2014, we decided to rent a place the next summer and to take Bill's family with us for a week. In the same neighborhood, we found a bigger, air-conditioned house to accommodate all seven of us: our immediate Malcolm family of four plus Bill's sister, her husband, and our nephew.

I woke up at 4:45 the first morning. I stood quietly next to my bed, thinking about where I could go and what I could do without waking the rest of the house. This search is not new to me. I'm the early riser whenever we go away. I've spent many mornings writing in hotel bathrooms, sitting on a chair with my feet propped up on the toilet.

That morning, I glanced at the stack of my books with my journal and pen lying on top. I saw the couch and the glass coffee table on the landing outside the bedrooms and in my head heard the heavy clank of my coffee mug. I saw chairs on the upper deck and imagined two sliding doors rumble through their tracks. Finally, I just sat motionless, reading on the couch in the carpeted living room, carefully placing my mug on the table so as not to clank it. At 6:00 a.m., I decide to make my exit. To the beach, taking with me my spiral-bound journal, a medium-point black pen, a mug of coffee, a blue bucket, and a folding chair.

I wrote in my journal. . . .

Today, on the way to the beach, I walk by the little cottage that we stayed in last year, and it sneers at me as if I am a traitor. I cross the boardwalk over the dunes and unfold my chair on soft sand. I drop everything on the chair, and I meander east on the beach to collect my favorite shells — jingle shells. With a handful of shells, I return to my chair and leave this section of sand to shy birds. A hopping sparrow pecks at the seaweed washed in overnight during high tide. A piping plover runs evenly with alternating feet along the hard wet pack. Where I sit, away from the immediate waterline, the piping plover looks like a clump of sand gliding across the beach.

Every beach along the coast has its own personality built by the cut of the shoreline, the topography of the land — perhaps dunes or just long stretches of sand, the creatures that live in and near the ocean, the treasures that the waves roll onto the beach — whether shells, sea glass, seaweed, or wood.

Here on Cape Cod, the most common shells are slipper shells, scallop shells, and jingle shells. Small, shiny, and opalescent, jingle shells gleam in the sunlight and cling to the sand after high tide. From being slightly cupped to roughly flat, they look and feel like fragile skeletons shed from the inside of bulkier shells. Surely nothing this delicate could have housed a creature to ride in the ofttimes rolling surf.

\*\*\*

This morning I pick up only jingle shells. As I shake a scant handful, they jingle together, acknowledging their name. And they look perfect in my hand, all in varying shades of yellow-orange, of slightly different shapes, and of varying sizes. The smallest is the size of a dime, and the largest is perhaps the size of a silver dollar. They are beautiful nestled together in my hand. How pretty they would be in a small glass bowl on the counter back at the house. I can add to the bowl after each seek.

A perfect display of shells. Perhaps I can drop the word *perfect* into the bowl with them. And leave it there. For that's about as far as that word really should be used. Where its expectations should halt. A perfect bowl of shells.

***

On the beach – it's the next day at 7 a.m. The jingle shell line has slipped into the ocean. I'm unsure if I missed it by an hour or need to wait an hour – is the tide coming in or going out?

That leaves me with the high tide seaweed to walk through. I tend to avoid shell seeking at this high waterline, preferring freshly rinsed shells planted along clean low-tide sand. But Jingle Shells are worth poking through this green slimy stuff.

Plus, I'm a bit more immune to seaweed today than I was yesterday. A local was overheard saying, "We've got the weed." In Colorado this would be understood differently than here on a Cape Cod beach. In Mom and Dad's garden in Iowa, it would have yet another meaning. And here, it means we have seaweed rolling onto the beach. I'm guessing a recent storm shook up the seaweed, and the waves have delivered it to our beach.

To swim, we walked out about ten feet through seaweed. Liam, who in the past has freaked out at the sight of seaweed, marched right through it. Thinking back, it was swimming through it that Liam didn't like. When it catches around your neck like a harness, and though you know there is no power in it, the slime around your neck feels lifelike and tugs as you swim. Swimming in deep water where you can't plant your feet and rise out of it, its force − however slight − is off-putting. Like the beginning of strangulation.

But this was seaweed around our knees, not our necks. Liam gathered it in his hands and formed balls. So I did, too. Then he squeezed it dry. I did the same, shivering at the sliminess of it. Then the game began. I underhanded a slow pitch, a big gangly lump of it, and Liam tried to knock it out of the air with a fast-pitched ball of the same. There was more than enough weed to keep this game going for an hour.

\*\*\*

A day later − the numbers associated with the days have disappeared. I was awake this morning at 7 o'clock to do my chores: pick up Jingle Shells on the beach. With an overcast sky, the beach doesn't look inviting.

The tide is going out, leaving me a wide, wet, watermarked area to comb. A row of Jingle Shell treasures at the farthest reach of the water's webbed fingers pulls me; then the row a bit lower tugs. Looking down the beach, I try to make a plan. I will walk a straight line on the top first, then return on the lower side.

It won't work. The Jingle Shells are rarer than slipper shells, and my head wags like a dog's tail scoping out both sides − which infuriates me, a woman who makes straight-ahead plans. Surely I can walk on a beach without a perfect plan. There's no need to keep on the straight and narrow. Must I fight by the sea that roaming urge that sabotages my daily land cruising?

No, today I'm looking left and right. Chasing bright shells and leaving whatever zigzag, straight, or diagonal path in my wake.

*** 

After that meandering walk yesterday in the morning sun, this morning opened with a bit of rain. By 9:30 a.m., it has cleared, and I walk to the beach. The Jingle Shell line is at the surf's edge, at the very point where incoming and outgoing waves meet and create a vacuum-like suction that leaves the shells rolling over my feet. Most are empty slippers. But the line is dotted with Jingle Shells.

These iridescent *Anomia simplex* bivalves lost a bit of their magic after Bill's sister, Anne, had a look through a Cape Cod shell book. She shared that they are also known as "toenail" shells and that they remind her of Bill's big toenail. Some twenty-odd years ago, Bill's buddy attached a bowling ball to Bill the night of his bachelor party. At one point, Bill dropped it on his big toe, and since then, it's never been the same. Yes, old toenails do look a bit like jingle shells.

To Anne's spoken observation, I called, "Objection! Retract!" for I don't want to collect old yellow toenails! But there it stuck. A couple years ago, I had a friend make beautiful necklaces for me using these delicate shells, and now I've promised Anne the most delightful piece of jewelry. Made only from the very best. The very biggest toenail shells. And the very yellowest.

*** 

A day after the Toenail Assertion, I'm working hard to reconfigure that statement − looking for a landing spot below absolute perfection of jingle shells and well above that of dead about-to-fall-off toenails. It didn't take much effort to reimagine the rough shells of apricot, yellow, and orange hues. Surely they must be mermaids' acrylic fingernails, beautiful yet marked by a vigorous undersea life. A tap on a rock or the peeling of lobster could surely pop off one of these brittle nails.

*** 

Our last evening . . . I wander back to the beach to gather my chair. I go without a bucket. I have enough shells. If I find more, I will take home only what fits nestled in my hand. At the sight of the water, I know I won't be shell seeking, for the tide is coming in strong. The water is reaching high sand that has been baking in the sun all day. My shell line is more than knee deep in the surf. I sit and watch the tide gather strength and push over the dry sand, bringing with it shreds of dead black seaweed. The big, green healthy clumps of it are gone. The pieces are now so small they look as if they've been pulsed in a blender.

I feel little. I realize that despite my not being on the beach tomorrow looking for Jingle Shells, they will still be here. The vastness of ocean and waves. Washing shells onto the beach. Leaving the same tidal lines I've worked all week.

I'm somber moving back inland.

# The Whale Tooth in the Trunk

At Wingaersheek Beach in Gloucester one day last July,
I picked up an intriguing skinny white foot-long stick.
At first, I thought it was just a hard piece of plastic. It
felt like the handle of a flyswatter but was frayed at one
end. Within 30 seconds, the thought of baleen whale
tooth came to mind. Where I pulled that from, God
only knows. I added it to the collection of shells I had
collected, near the beach quilt under the blue and white
beach umbrella – our beach camp.

At the end of the day, we packed our sandy beach
chairs, coolers, quilt, and buckets into the van. And
added one *possible* whale tooth.

At home, I shook out the blankets, put the chairs
and buckets in the garage, and took the coolers to the
mudroom. I knew what to do with those items in our
day-at-the-beach inventory. But a potential whale tooth?
I gave it an up-close inspection. Hard plastic on one end
and split into thin plastic hairs at the other. I went into
the house and Googled *baleen whale tooth*. Sure enough,
that's what it was, well, more or less: I discovered that
technically baleen whales don't have teeth; I had found
a *baleen plate*. In December, what I considered to be my
whale tooth was still in the back of my van.

Why was it still there? Well, where does one keep
an amazing treasure like a whale tooth? It wouldn't fit
in my shell jar; plus, that was meant for shells only. It

might have fit in the long, rectangular bronze planter box perched high on top of the computer hutch. That's where I keep the complete horseshoe crab shells I've collected. A long way from the ocean, they are tucked deep into the planter, collecting dust from the air. They share the planter with a small creeping plant lodged at one end.

As I think about it, a leathery mermaid's purse had also landed in that planter. I found it while beachcombing in Cape Ann; it was caught up in seaweed left behind at high tide. Mermaid's purses are egg cases of shark or skate embryos. About four to six inches long, these tough cases protect and feed embryos up to fifteen months before they hatch. When I first found this empty mermaid's purse, I thought it was a strange beetle. It was black and pod-shaped with a set of spikes on either end. There was a hatching hole on the back side. The mermaid's purse was a true treasure.

I know why I didn't put the whale tooth into the planter. It's a silly place to keep a treasure. I wanted to see it – as I would like to see the horseshoe crab shells and the mermaid's purse. However, I know that scattering my beach memorabilia willy-nilly on shelves will put them in a whole new category – no longer Treasure but rather Clutter. Collectors of Dust. A better home decorator would have sussed this out sooner.

I had a thought. I could put the odd-shaped sea treasures in a clear, oblong glass serving plate that I have tucked away, then put it on display on a shelf. When the treasures and the glass gather dust, I could just run them under water to give them a quick cleaning. But this mini–beach vignette wouldn't appear until Christmas decorations had spent time on that shelf, so the safest place for the whale tooth was still in the back of my van. What was one more month with a whale tooth stuck in the trunk?

# A Hairy Tale

On a warm summer day in July 2013, I embarked on my first deep-sea fishing trip with my good friend Kim, who grew up in Michigan. Our birthdays are a day apart, and we have decided to celebrate with shared experiences rather than physical gifts. One year, we picked cranberries from a bog, and in another, we took an all-day cheese-making class. This particular year, we were going out from Gloucester on a deep-sea fishing charter.

I had high hopes for this trip. I wanted to bring home my first fish from this aquatic farmland called the Atlantic and eat it for dinner. The challenging logistics of fishing that had played out on the Annisquam River would not be an issue on this boat. The captain or his mates would be there to take the fish off the line and then gut and fillet it for me. I tried to keep an open mind to the type of fish I might catch. Codfish, haddock, pollack, cusk, wolffish, redfish, mud hake, and conger eel were all possibilities according to the boat's website. But I wholeheartedly wanted codfish.

The first cod I ever ate was from the Schwan's man's truck in the 1970s. The brown freezer truck would stop at our farm every couple of weeks. The Schwan's man, as well known as the UPS man, would bring a color trifold brochure to the door. Depending on the inventory remaining from the last stop, Mom would buy a gallon of butter brickle ice cream, a box of breaded pork tenderloin patties, breaded shrimp, or cod fillets. Mom would thaw and bake those frozen bricks of whitefish with a little lemon pepper.

I probably tasted true fresh cod, not previously frozen, when I first went to England with Bill in 1989. Fish and chips is a convenient fast-food English meal from the local "chippy," the fish-and-chip shop. In more recent years here in Massachusetts, I've bought cod from our local fresh fish counters. But with a deep-sea fishing trip, the ultimate was possible: to catch my own codfish and, within four hours, have it for dinner.

The charter boat would set sail at 3:30 p.m. and return at 8 p.m. We Malcolms had a relaxing Sunday morning at home. Around 2 p.m., I thought I should get showered and dressed. I skipped washing my hair, thinking it would just get blown to shreds on the boat. I skipped most of my makeup, too. I tossed a baseball cap into my backpack; then I found an extra one and tossed it in for Kim, along with an extra long-sleeved thermal shirt for her.

When I picked Kim up, I was shocked by her appearance. She had done her hair, put on makeup – and she even smelled good! I said something like, "We're going fishing – you know that, right?"

The boat was bigger than I expected. It was at least fifty feet long. At the very front of the boat, we staked out two fishing rod holders that were made of short PVC pipes bound to the rail of the boat. Out of thirty-five people, Kim and I, along with six Japanese tourists, were the only ones who stayed out on deck at the bow as we left the harbor. Most passengers were huddled quietly in the cabin, looking as if they were going into a coal mine. No laughter, no chatting.

We couldn't have asked for a more perfect day. Sunny and only two-foot waves. The boat glided out of the harbor toward the open Atlantic. At the mouth of the harbor, another fishing charter boat was coming in. The grinning captain tooted and waved to our boat. We waved back, and seconds later we plowed into that boat's wake. Our bow created a spectacular ten-foot spray that showered us and our Japanese counterparts.

Kim's curls were washed away. I turned to look at the crow's nest, and through my seawater-drenched hair, I saw our captain chortling behind the window of his wheelhouse. I told Kim I had an extra cap and shirt, but she opted for the extra layer of warmth over the cap.

We motored an hour out to where the waters were two hundred feet deep. The captain dropped anchor. We watched one of the ship's mates as he showed a woman across the bow from us how to get set up. Our bait was sea clams that we wove onto the hooks with three pokes. The reels were what I would call open-fly: with a flick of a lever, the line comes whizzing out as the one-gram weight pulls the baited hook to the bottom of the ocean, where cod spend most of their time. Back on our side of the bow, I watched Kim go through the steps of dropping the line; then I followed suit.

The captain descended from his splash tower. "That made your day, didn't it?" we ribbed him.

"You bet it did!" he replied.

We bantered with the captain, the two mates, and the loveliest fisherman named Paddy, who shared the bow with us. Paddy, probably in his seventies, had his own gear and bait, and a big, confident cooler to store his catch. A bit shy at first, Paddy was one of those guys who would be a great neighbor. Kind, polite, and good-hearted. He gave us a couple of pointers along the way, and he had the corner on big fish at the end of the day, landing a two-foot codfish.

Kim and I waited for a nibble. I told the captain that I had grown up in Iowa, where we used bobbers on lakes and rivers. Without a bobber, I wasn't sure what to watch for. He reached out to the end of my pole and gave the line a couple little tugs to show us what it felt like when something went after the bait. With the line locked in place on the reel, I held the line between my fingers so I could feel it move in addition to the pole when something bit.

Three feet apart on the bow, Kim and I chatted and laughed, I with my cap and she with her now-uncurled hair blowing in the wind. All rods were quiet, not much happening. We saw a small codfish come in, but it was only fifteen inches, and they need to be nineteen inches to keep. Then tug, tug! Fish on my line! I started to reel it in as the captain came in our direction.

"Where's your camera?" shouted Kim as she reached for my coat pocket. I was so focused on pull, reel, pull, reel that I could hardly talk.

"Pocket!" I replied.

"Which one?" Kim asked as she reached across me to the far coat pocket.

In my frenzy to get dinner on board, I could not say "jean pocket." And I couldn't let go of my pole to get the camera out myself.

"Don't worry about the camera, Linda. Just keep reeling and get that fish on board!" directed the captain.

Then came Kim's direction: "NO! NO! DON'T REEL! MY HAIR'S CAUGHT IN YOUR REEL!!"

Thankfully, Kim wasn't in pain. I would have felt horrible if she was suffering, for I was losing strength from laughter that made my whole body shake. My cheeks were so scrunched up in the fit that I didn't see how the captain released Kim's hair. I only heard his voice saying, "OK, Linda! Now! Reel it in!"

Still weak with laughter, I reeled and reeled and reeled until finally Kim yelled, "It's a shark!"

Yes, I had nabbed myself a dogfish. An inedible, two-foot-long slender sharklike fish. After a brief photo, the ship's mate, who had taken it off my line, released it, saying it was no good to eat. Paddy told us they release urine throughout their body if they aren't cleaned right, so the meat tastes like ammonia. But, he said, in England they were used in fish and chips. I'm unsure if there is any truth to that or any of the many fish stories we heard that day, but I'm absolutely sure of the hair-in-reel one.

After that episode, the captain declared, "I've been doing this for thirty years and have never seen that before."

Paddy summed it up best: "You two girls are having the most fun out of everyone on this boat!"

We didn't catch dinner, and we came home smelling as if we had been clamming, not fishing. But we'd had a wicked good time. I wonder how the captain and his mates told the story.

# Simple Squid Dinner

For dinner one Monday night, I had leftover ingredients from the weekend to work with: a bowl of overripe tomatoes, an onion, some garlic, two lemons, a handful of linguine, a bottle of Chardonnay, and one and a half pounds of squid. The squid was left over from the paella Bill had made Saturday night.

Spanish paella is one of Bill's spectacular, layered creations in the kitchen. Starting with a quick stir-fry of chicken, pork, onions, peppers, garlic – and sometimes squid – he adds rice, chopped tomatoes, and chicken broth with saffron; puts the cover on; and lets the rice fully cook. Then he stacks seafood on top of the rice, covers it once more, and keeps it on the heat for ten minutes to steam the clams, mussels, and shrimp. Then, as a grand finale, Bill carries the heavy wok from the stove to the table, whips the lid off, and immediately sprinkles roasted pine nuts over the top. It's an impressive entrée for guests.

Working with leftovers from that event, I rustled through my online recipe box looking for an easy tomato and white wine sauce that I had made a few weeks before. With a quick search for *squid*, a stuffed squid recipe popped up. Opening the bag of porcelain sleek and glossy white squid tubes, I decided that stuffing them would be a ridiculous endeavor. Instead, I quickly chopped them up. A deconstructed squid dish. Think

Indiana Jones in battle with a foolhardy, impractical whip when a quick shot seemed to make more sense.

Thankfully, all the skin, ink, and cartilage was gone before said squid had entered our house. I was left with long white tubes and even longer purple tentacles. I chopped the squid tubes into calamari rings and threw them into a strainer to rinse. I picked up the tentacles, some four to six inches long, and put them into the strainer as well.

As the tentacles hung in front of my nose, I murmured, "I'm a heck of a long way from Iowa."

I didn't have time to soak the pieces in milk to tenderize them. I didn't get the meat tenderizing hammer out because I didn't want squid juice squirting all over my clean counter and floor. Instead I decided they would just need to tenderize as they simmered away in tomatoes, onions, garlic, and wine for ten minutes.

As the ingredients came to a happy simmer, I peeked inside one last time before putting the cover on the pan. I was puzzled by the bizarreness of these little creatures, prepared by my Iowa-born hands, smothered in a Creole-infused sauce. Would Granddad Bauer have eaten these? He loved fish, but this was a far cry from beer-battered bullheads. Would my dad knowingly eat these? Dad had *unknowingly* eaten them when we ordered fried calamari rings once while he was visiting. We didn't tell him the source of the nice rubbery, crunchy appetizer.

The end result of this simmered squid, served over rice, was delicious. A purple tentacle waved to me just before I ate it. And that conflicted, elusive sensation washed over me again. Am I an Iowa farm girl or a Yankee woman? Can I be both?

# Mother-in-Law's Tongue and Christmas Cactus

<hr/>

With nights that dip into the low 40s, the houseplants that have spent the summer on our porch deck are moving inside. I have only a few plants, and I call them heirloom plants: a mother-in-law tongue from Grandma Bauer, a climbing vine from Granddad Bauer's funeral, a giant Christmas cactus from Grandma Mills, and a "puppy" Christmas cactus started from a big piece that broke off of that giant. In 2005, I drove these plants 1,600 miles to Massachusetts when Will was a toddler.

For years, the mother-in-law's tongue has never been that healthy or prolific under my care. I couldn't even get the leaves to stand up straight. I've had wooden chopsticks snugly tied with twine around the tall spiked leaves to keep them cinched straight up.

The leaves are dark green from age. They look fragile. Tired. I moved the plant to the deck for the summer, and I removed the sticks and the twine. The plant was in a corner where there was room for it to splay its leaves a bit.

A few days later, I hovered over it with the watering can. Looking into the middle of the plant, where all those spikes radiated from, I saw a short, light-green point.

In all my attempts to help the plant stand up straight, I had been suffocating it. New growth erupts from the middle. The place I had committed to darkness with the leaves pulled together so tightly with twine string that kept out any sun or air that might have generated a young spike years ago.

With water, it lived. With the untying of the string, it's thriving.

The grand matriarch that made the journey east is the big Christmas cactus from my dad's mom, Grandma Mills. Grandma estimated that it must have been at least 125 years old. It had belonged to her mother long before it moved into Grandma's house. We did that math more than twenty years ago. When Grandma was in her eighties, she left the farm and moved into an apartment in town. That's when the cactus and the walnut stand where it perches moved to Illinois with me. Its tendrils bloomed beautifully in Grandma's house. Bunches and bunches of pink flowers.

These are the bits of care trivia I gleaned from Grandma: Give it castor oil in October and leave it root-bound. In my care, I'm happy to say it stayed green and had an occasional bud when we lived in Illinois. However, since I moved to Massachusetts in 2005, it has sat stubbornly for fourteen years, without a single bloom. Perhaps because I didn't believe in the castor oil tale. Or perhaps because one year I tried olive oil instead. I thought Grandma said any oil would work.

Last spring, I had to do something. That cactus didn't look healthy. The 135-year-old limbs were wedged into the pot. Had it ever been re-potted? I bought a pot double the size of what it was in. Then I looked at that new pot for a couple weeks. Dare I do it? I lifted the terracotta pot out of the basket. I was wowed. The terracotta pot was beautiful. In all the years I had the cactus, I had never seen this pot. If I lost the cactus as a result of this re-potting, I still had this pot, but unfortunately, none of its history. Had Grandma ever seen this hand-painted piece of art?

Why is the thought of re-potting a plant more complicated than the actual job? In minutes, I had dropped the root-bound old lady into fresh dirt and placed her on the table. With her drooping leaves, she still looked miserable.

Then summer came, and she could not spew shiny new leaves fast enough! Really, really beautiful. If she was putting all that effort into growing over the summer, I felt obliged to work out what she needed when she came inside.

I spent a good hour scouring the internet trying to find the secret: "how to get a Christmas cactus to bloom." The most concise and scientific information was from one horticulturist who gloated that if you know what you are doing, it's really not that difficult. Light and temperature are key.

Christmas cacti rely on the light of the environment to determine when to bloom. Photoperiodism. To force blooms, and to put photoperiodism into motion, the cactus needs twelve hours of absolute darkness for six to eight weeks before she will bloom. Sources give sound advice: move it into a dark closet or bathroom every night and bring it out every morning. This matriarch fills nearly three cubic feet of space. Lugging her around morning and night won't work.

Christmas cacti rely on cool nights – ideally 50 to 55 degrees – for the same period of time that it is dark. Reading this reminded me how cold Grandma's extra bedroom used to be. The only autumn guest was this cactus. In our house, between the baseboard heating in one zone of the first floor and the radiant heat in the other zone, temps rarely drop below 70 degrees.

Neither Bill nor I was completely convinced we could close off a hallway for eight weeks to give this matriarch a nice dark space. Bill suggested putting her in the laundry room. I balked as I spend half my life in there, but that's where she landed. The open-plan laundry room was reduced to a walk-in and back-out galley-style laundry room. It felt like doing laundry with a happy green English sheepdog gently nudging my backside. But allowances must be made for six to eight weeks.

Nightly at 6 p.m., I slid the hallway door to the laundry room shut in order to block the light from HRC (Her Royal Cactus). I cut, flattened, and taped two brown paper bags together, trying to create a kind of blanket for HRC to block light from the other end of the hallway that leads to the kitchen. I needed at least two more bags as this blanket covered only the top third of her. Early the next morning, I saw the light from our neighbors' back porch out the laundry room window.

Could this sleeping beauty see it? Did it distract her? If only she could have said. I could get a pole, lodge it between two shelves, and hang a temporary curtain.

The first night, I cranked the small window wide open to give her fresh air, to make the air she breathed stay below 55 degrees. I closed the baseboard heater in the laundry room. When my alarm went off at 6 a.m., I hit a thermocline halfway down the stairs. My tired head immediately calculated adjustments to help the Malcolms and HRC acclimate to one another: crank the window shut a bit and turn on the heat in all zones. The second morning, the brisk chill was limited to the laundry room.

It was a long, dark incubation season – that led to no blooms. But still, each summer, HRC grows and grows more green leaves. And stubbornly, HRC still refuses to do any more than that. This grand matriarch is high maintenance, and she takes up a lot of space when she moves indoors for the winter. She continues to be green and healthy but without a single flower.

# Sniffs

What with all that's different between my sister Leslie and me, we have a few bizarre similarities. All the more remarkable because we live over 1,600 miles apart. We both used the same hair straightener before my hair went permanently curly when it grew back after chemo in 2010. Occasionally, we have the same brand and style of purse. And a few years ago, we both discovered linens from Grandma Mills's house in our own homes, on the same Sunday afternoon. We did the same thing. Hoped. And lifted them to our noses.

I knew the purple satin pajamas would not smell like Grandma's. I've had them a long time and had sniffed them before. Leslie's was a surprise bag – a big black garbage bag full of miscellaneous towels and clothes. She smelled a turtleneck, and there it was. She wrapped it up and put it back into the bag quickly. We talked three days later and were a little freaked out when we realized we had been sniffing on the same day. Leslie promised I could smell the turtleneck when I visited.

Later at her house, she opened the bag quickly, took a deep sniff, and gave the turtleneck to me. It was there. We quickly shuffled through the bag, looking for more. A finger towel I had given to Dad's mom years ago was still fragrant. Not wanting the smell to evaporate, Leslie quickly wrapped it in a third towel and put the bundle in a Ziploc bag. The third towel was a protective barrier against the smell of the baggie. I carried it in my hand luggage from Mitchellville to Cedar Rapids to Chicago to Boston. Anxious about losing it, I continually checked on it throughout the trip.

Breathing it in sends me time traveling. I'm home visiting, staying with my brother and his family in town, about five minutes from Grandma's apartment. I call Dad the night before and say, "I'll go see Grandma in the morning." The next morning, I roll out of bed, put clothes on, and go to Grandma's apartment. The door is unlocked, which means she's awake. She probably dressed in the dark and wheeled herself to the living room at 3 a.m. Then I'm sitting in Grandpa's old recliner, Portmeirion Botanic Garden coffee mug in hand, immersed in the smell of her apartment. She says that she thought my dad would have been there by now. I tell her that I had told Dad that she and I were going to visit that morning. On her face is disappointment glazed with gratitude for my being there. I don't feel underappreciated. Grandma wants what she wants when she wants it.

I hesitate to call it a smell or to say I sniffed it. It's more of a living remnant from a life that left earth over thirteen years ago. A breath of life that is gone. A haunting. One that I daren't visit too often; after all, how many sniffs are in there? I don't want to use all of them up. Don't want to breathe it in too greedily.

The gift of my nose. If I'm ever bedridden, I've thought about what I want under my nose as I take my last breaths: lilacs, cilantro, Johnson's baby soap, and now, those finger towels.

Thirteen years after Grandma died, I am enjoying a cup of coffee in my Portmeirion Botanic Garden coffee mug. Hand washed daily, it hasn't met its demise. When we have houseguests, I put it away in the china hutch. When it breaks, I will cry. I don't want someone else to break it and think they are the cause of my tears.

My sister's turtleneck was accidentally washed. When she came out to see me, I offered her half of my sniffs. She declined as she held the towel to her nose. She said there weren't enough left to share.

# April Fresh Scent

Shakespeare's time was before toothbrushes, deodorant, and regular bathing. So people did what they could: wash underwear as often as they could afford, use scented waters and perfumes, and carry nosegays. Throughout the 1980s, Mom made silk flower bouquets for brides, so I know *nosegay* as a very small handheld bouquet. Its presence in the 1500s was the same size, perhaps even just a single fragrant flower. While in crowds of people, all of whom probably had some degree of body odor, the nosegay was held under the nose to help block the unpleasantries.

I have used similar tactics as a parent. I recall a late summer festival a few years ago at Stage Fort Park in Gloucester, Massachusetts. The park is a long, sprawling green area right on the ocean. The parking lot was across the road from our starting point, the playground. After swinging, climbing, and teeter-tottering, we moved to the outdoor car show adjacent to the playground. Bill tried to lure the boys to and through antique, or muscle, or exotic cars. To me they were all just shiny vehicles with four wheels. Meanwhile, I noticed small tents set up in rows just beyond the food booths. An art show. A wide selection of potential made-in-the-USA Christmas gifts for family and friends in England.

We needed to make our way through lunch and through those food booths to go shopping. The outdoor food aroma was reminiscent of the smells of pork chop sandwiches at the Buchanan County Fair in Independence, Iowa, or fried dough and cotton candy sweetening the air at the Topsfield Fair in Massachusetts. Here, hugging the Atlantic, the aroma was undoubtedly that of fried clams. Strips or bellies. The smell pulled me like that of corn dogs when I was little – when the carnival rides and food trucks filled the main street in my hometown, and I split the dollars in my pocket between Tilt-A-Whirl rides and those fried dogs on sticks, in that order.

Will couldn't bear to go near the intoxicated atmosphere surrounding the food booths. His sensitive nose smelled a repulsive enemy in those fried clams. We stayed on the outskirts of the food booths, staking out a spot near the ocean to picnic. Then Bill dove headlong into that clam haven and emerged with fries for Will and Liam and a basket of clams for him and me to share. We put space between the clams and the fries, but even now, the complaints about the smell drown out the memory of the taste of those fried clams.

As we finished lunch, I again eyed the art fair. We could get there only by walking through the air that was soaked with fried clams. I told Will to hold his French fries to his nose. We made it through the festival with this improvised nosegay. It was a condensed shopping trip. For the boys, shopping was ranked just below the smell of clams.

Before driving home, we took a bathroom break. I followed a stream of women toward the park's main bathroom. Then, with the wind in the perfect direction, I smelled the sweetest scent. It was from the past. I had missed it. I closely followed the woman in front of me while we stood in line, breathing in her trailing air. It wasn't an expensive perfume. It wasn't the nostalgic detergent smell of Grandma Mills's apartment in Iowa years ago. It was the April fresh scent of fabric softener.

Liam has had eczema since he was a baby, so I did double duty, washing adult clothes in regular detergent followed by a fabric softener rinse, and using only a baby detergent for our two young sons' laundry. During their preschool years, I met another mom who mentioned an allergen-free, environmentally friendly laundry detergent that would work for all Malcolms. I immediately halved the loads of laundry done in one week by washing everyone's clothes together. I became accustomed to the smell of nothingness in our clean laundry. Our clothes are clean, but there is no fresh scent residue when they come out of the dryer.

Months after this Gloucester visit, we skied during February break, and the place where we stayed laundered the towels and sheets using a fabric softener in the rinse. With a week of fresh-smelling linens, I decided to take action. Towels and sheets for the master bedroom would be rinsed in a little bit of fabric softener. Not a lot. Just enough.

In the washer, the agitator has a cup on top labeled, "Pour in one capful of fabric softener." A big jug of fabric softener from years past sat in the laundry room. Bottom shelf of the baker's rack, tucked in the back. I dusted off the bottle and took off the lid. A gentle tip of the heavy bottle produced a thick blue slug peering out of the bottle.

In Grandma Mills's words of disgust, "Oooo-gah!"

In Great-Grandma Whittier's words of frugality, "Waste not, want not."

In replicating Grandma Bauer's practicality, driven by her mother and teacher Great-Grandma Whittier, I was not long disgusted or perplexed. I brought to the laundry room a two-cup Pyrex measuring cup and a small whisk. A two-inch blue slug flopped into the bottom of the cup. With the addition of a half cup of water and a brisk whisk, the slug melted into a more familiar blue state. A scant quarter cup went in with the load of towels. When they sprang from the dryer, they were again, at long last, April fresh.

The 64-ounce bottle of concentrated slugs should last at least a year.

# The American Laundry Maven

Seven days in a small house as hurricane winds and flooding rains sweep through the London area a few days before Christmas is when "quaint" converts to "cramped."

Our playground away from home, the cricket pitch, became a green swamp, and the wicked winds kept gusting for days after the thrashing storm blew away. But for the occasional walk around the block, we were stuck inside.

For seven days, cabin fever hit hard. Yet, the American Laundry Maven didn't get bored. Nearly every day, she gathered a small load of dirty clothes in her washtub or mini–laundry basket and trooped it downstairs to the kitchen to load the washer.

She stuffed the armful of clothing through a small door that opened to a small cavern. The Maven pushed Go but skipped the Rinse Hold cycle. Instead of having it sit in rinse water overnight, she let the load spin out immediately, surely breaking an English Laundry Law as the clothes gathered more wrinkles than the law allows.

For years on these visits, the American Laundry Maven has taken her laundry to the dryer in the garage. But on this trip, the wind and the rain guided her toward the more traditional drying apparatus: the Rack. Using the dryer, which would result in soft, foldable clothes didn't seem feasible in blustery 90 mph gales. It was strange enough on a dry day heading out the back door with the mini-basket, through the gate, across the back garden, through the outer gate, unlocking the garage, opening it, then flicking on the switch so electricity flowed to the dryer. Plus now, with all the rain, the garden path was crunchy with snails.

No, this time around, the Rack seemed less torturous. As if planned, the load that fit in the mini-basket fit in the washer and fit on the Rack. Preferably next to a radiator, overnight the clothes would get pretty dry. Before the Maven hung them on the Rack, she gave them an intense shake to knock out some of the wrinkles.

The next stop for the laundry the following morning was the airing cupboard, which is a cuddly, warm little closet where the water heater lives wrapped up in a thermal blanket. Yet another wooden Rack, a folded one, stands in front of the heater. And this is the laundry's destination after the freestanding Rack.

The Maven takes the clothes from the Rack, carefully presses out more wrinkles with her hands before folding each item in half and meticulously draping them over the Folded Rack, then closes the door. It's a kind of low-temp kiln. Several hours in there completes the drying process.

The next morning, when Will says, "I can't find any pants," the Maven knows she has washed them, so she backtracks. Hanging near a radiator? On the Rack? Ahh, the hiding place, the Folded Rack in the airing cupboard. She emerges a hero as she shakes a few more wrinkles out and hands Will warm pants.

And at that moment, the American Laundry Maven breaks English Laundry Law yet again: She does not iron the clothes that came out of the airing cupboard. But no one suspects a thing. And the Maven has been doing this for a week without the English Laundry Maven next door stealing dry laundry to iron.

Really, the American Laundry Maven would much prefer that the English Laundry Maven put her feet up and have a cup of tea than iron the American Laundry Maven's clothes.

# Swordfish with Tomatoes and Capers

My go-to summertime, never-fail fish recipe is Ina Garten's "Swordfish with Tomatoes and Capers." I've made a couple of Linda Malcolm tweaks to it. First, no capers because Bill is allergic to them. Second, I've only ever used home-canned tomatoes. Mom's pints of canned tomatoes, which traveled 1,600 miles to my house by van, became not only a simple chili sauce but, more impressively, a New England swordfish sauce.

When I ran out of Mom's pints, my friend Kate and I turned the heat up in my kitchen and canned our own tomatoes. I was unsure if I would have been brave enough to can on my own, but that was a special day – a replica of an Iowa summer day when friends and aunts visit to help can or freeze bushels of vegetables and fruit. As I see it, unless you have home-canned tomatoes, my tomato sauce is unduplicatable, for it's hard to get the same magic from a store-bought can of tomatoes whose preparer you've never met.

This recipe is perfect for a foodie who loves to cook but still wants to enjoy the company of guests and not be hovering over the stove while guests chat with your backside. First, an early morning trip for the fresh swordfish catch at our local grocery store. Here, the fish counter is as long as the red meat counter at Fareway grocery stores in Iowa.

A few hours before dinner, in a large high-sided skillet, flavors are coaxed out over time through layers of ingredients — onions and leeks pop in olive oil, followed by the mingling of garlic. Then tomatoes, salt, and pepper. Minutes later, wine and chicken stock join the orchestra. I cook the sauce through a ten-minute simmer; then I take it off the heat. Later, when the swordfish goes on the grill, I bring the tomato and fennel magic back to a simmer and finish it off with basil and butter.

Rather than a 28-ounce can of drained plum tomatoes that the recipe calls for, I use two pints of undrained home-canned tomatoes. As I pop the lids, my ritualistic sniff confirms the tomatoes are still good — or not. Saturday afternoon, sadly, I had only three remaining jars of tomatoes. I was making dinner for four. I recognized one jar as mine, canned with Kate two years earlier in September of 2013. Its fresh hit to my nose confirmed its goodness. The second lid was unmarked, and the tomatoes were a slightly darker red. I popped it open, sniffed, questioned, and sniffed again. Borderline. If I had been cooking only for Bill and me, I would've used it, but I didn't want to take the risk of poisoning guests.

I reached to the back of the shelf for jar number three. Oh my — it was one of those edgy jars with the two-digit year written on the lid. I didn't even open it; instead, I moved ahead with a little extra chicken stock in the pot. Dinner was good, but I could tell the tomato sauce wasn't two pints deep. It wasn't as good as the week before when I'd made swordfish for a party of eight – with four pints of my canned tomatoes.

Why didn't I open the third pint? It was either from '90 or '06, depending on which way you turned the jar to read the year on the lid. I envisioned thirty pints of cooled canned tomatoes on Mom's counter and her Sharpie quickly swiping the year on each lid. Logically, I think the year was '06 because they had driven out to see me in '07 with boxes of canned beans and tomatoes in the cargo hold. Then there is a little part of me that wants to believe it might have been from '90 and managed to survive hundreds of miles on the road and many, many years spinning on the Lazy Susan in my corner cupboard.

(An aside: If you want your mom to call you, just mention in an email that you are considering eating a pint of her canned tomatoes that might be twenty years old. The phone rings minutes after pushing Send.)

The last swordfish supper of the full-tomato version marked the visit of Midwest friends we hadn't seen in a couple of years. I remember them sitting around our dining room table and thinking how amazing it was to have them with us. Sixteen hundred miles they had flown just a few hours before, and here they sat at our table for dinner. Surreal. The last supper of the half-tomato version was for local friends whom we see more often, their faces around our table more familiar. The laughter and conversations from time spent with both sets of friends echo over the empty Ball jars on the open shelves in my kitchen.

# Rock-Hard Resilience

Early one spring, I helped my son Liam's den fulfill one of their elective badges as Webelos II in Cub Scouts. I led a couple days' worth of activities about rocks. At the first meeting in a classroom, we talked about the great Pangaea, when all the continents nestled together, and the scouts plowed folded beach towels together to simulate plate tectonics crashing and forming mountains. We spread chocolate frosting on paper plates and slid graham crackers against one another on top of it to simulate plates at a fault line. The chocolate was the molten lava on which the plates floated.

The second meeting was at the ocean's edge in Marblehead, Massachusetts, to examine volcanic rock. It was a shocking discovery for this Midwesterner to discover that my current home sits on igneous rock from 550 million years ago. Ironically, where I grew up in Northeast Iowa, fossilized limestone is prevalent – a result of Iowa being covered by shallow seas about the same time as the volcanoes were active here in Marblehead.

Our first stop was Devereux Beach, where all the rock was formed thousands of feet below the Earth's surface. Having been rolled by the waves, the granite rocks on the beach were smooth. We found beautiful xenoliths in rocks, where magma cooled and ensnared other minerals. A mile from this beach, we climbed

Castle Rock and watched the high-tide waves crash into the sides of it. Jutting upward, yellowish rhyolite and black basalt heaved in what were the sides of a very old volcano. The rock dome, being some 30-feet high, was jagged. The dome's height protected it from the pounding surf, unlike the smooth rocks at the beach.

The day after our outing, my eye caught something unusual on the floor under the living room window. It was a five-pound intrusive igneous granite rock with a beautiful gray-white xenolith running through it. Hauled in by Liam from our trip to the beach, it was tucked into a vignette of plants on two small tables. The rock grounded the scene.

At the top of the stairs going to our bedrooms, beach treasures rest on a hall table, including six small rocks from a beach in Kingston, Massachusetts. My collection of heart-shaped rocks is in this mix, too. All of them are smooth – as though for years they had been sent rolling on the sand by wave after relentless wave.

I walk down the stairs of the deck and see in the flower garden to the left a line of smooth rocks that our family has collected from Cape Ann beaches over the twelve years we've lived here.

Why do I collect rocks? They are visual reminders of places I've been. Plus, their smoothness is comforting. Their mass is solid. They have been through a giant rock tumbler that has left them far from their original state, and this new form is beautiful.

They wouldn't be this way without every hurricane that threw them onto the rocky shoreline, every giant wave that rolled them on the ocean floor, every grain of sand that scratched them.

# The Commonality between Cat's Cradle and Crossback Bras

———◆———

Early one June, I dug out the few sleeveless tops I had and the one crossback bra that miraculously made the crisscross support straps disappear under said tops. With summer coming, I needed to add a few pieces to this small warm-weather wardrobe. Following a strong coffee, two ibuprofen, and a pep talk from a friend, I made my way into the mall.

I planned to have three full hours in this place: two to find shirts and one to find bras for under the shirts. This plan was derived from lessons learned during the previous summer's less-well-strategized shopping trips. On the first trip, I found the most delightful summery bras. One had bright pink stripes, and another had beautiful plum and yellow stripes. They were a far cry from my normal beige. A couple weeks later, I went on a second trip to shop for tops, and I was quite successful in finding light-colored cotton tops with my signature necklines that scoop or are V-shaped.

I'm not one to plan my outfit for the next day before I go to bed. At seven the following morning, excited by my new purchases gathered in those two outings, I pulled a spring mint-green V-neck over my head and stepped back to see my reflection in the full-length mirror. Then, I counted the pink stripes on my bra.

Through the shirt. My entire summer wardrobe was mismatched: the light colors and material of the shirts were translucent to the screaming striped bras.

With these lessons in mind, I searched out brightly patterned V-necks and scooped tops. Those necklines work best with my round face, and patterned fabrics camouflage my post–breast cancer uneven bust. The selection of tops included a few sleeveless styles, and I needed a new crossback bra, so I took my shopping bag directly from the top shop to the bra shop, determined not to create the wardrobe malfunction of last year.

I knew the size and the style I wanted in the bra: the exact same crossback style as the old one at home. At the display case, I threw open my shirt bag and worked at color coordination. Finding three beige bras that would potentially work, I decided to try them on with the tops just to confirm. It had been an expensive goof the previous year.

Peering into the puzzle of straps and holes, and judging where my arms and head must go, I had forgotten the game a woman must play getting into a crossback bra: cat's cradle – the string game played with two players. As you create the cradle and pass it back and forth between two sets of fingers, one slip and that's it. There's no recovery, and the string must be restrung to play again.

When one looks into that upside-down crossback bra, the view is the same as the one requiring a player to go into the cat's cradle, pinch the *X*'s, and bring them out, up, and under the outer strings, taking the string off their partner's fingers with just the right tension. Getting a crossback bra on is equally as complicated. Only it's played naked – and alone.

I studied the path, knowing only too well that I hadn't done this since last summer. Focusing, I saw the two holes to either side where my arms must go and the one in the middle, at the bottom of the $X$, for my head. Taking a moment and a small breath, I dove in. My head and left arm shot through the left armhole. Instantaneously, I was ensnared.

Two clear visions of possibility struck me: to simply to take my head out of the armhole and put it through the head hole, or to hit the call button and get some help. Neither was good: the first impossible and the second too embarrassing. I needed to heave the tight elastic contraption completely over my head and start again.

Trembling in the tight enclosure, my eyes glanced up to the mirror where I saw myself looking petrified. Given how and where my limbs were caught, I resembled a trapped animal about to attempt an improbable escape. I looked like a woman who had just been told she had breast cancer and was trying to escape from those words. This was not that, I convinced myself. Days of dread and fear reflecting back from the mirror were behind me. I was simply stuck in a piece of fashion apparatus.

With force, I pushed the bra up and pulled my arms and head out, slingshotting the bra against the opposite wall and watching it drop to the floor. I was shaking slightly as attempt number two resulted in twisted straps. I again disentangled, easier this time. On the third attempt, the cobwebs of autumn and winter fell aside, and I succeeded in summer's first game of cat's cradle.

Ready for the heat and humidity of summer, I knew not to try any quick readjustment techniques from twisted straps or misplacement of limb or head, for there was no recovery. The string must always be restrung.

# Scrabble Grandma

One morning in June 2013, Grandma Bauer, Mom's mom, started her journey Home. Grandma was ninety-five years old. She had been ill in April of that year but had beat two rounds of lung infections and then a bout with an intestinal virus. Her body was tired. My cousin called her "Apple Grandma" because they often made apple pies together. I remember making pies with Grandma, too. But to me, she was "Scrabble Grandma." After Sunday dinners, the Scrabble board would come out, dictionary and all.

The shadow of time smoothed over the Sundays as they progressed through my lifetime from her Scrabble tile rack shared with me; to my Scrabble rack shared with her; to our individual tile racks with a bit of help at the end of the game; to pretty fierce competitors, each of us manning our respective tile rack right to the end of the game.

Through my year of breast cancer, I savored the moment when Grandma and I could sit across the table and play Scrabble again. But by the time I traveled back to Iowa after all of that, Grandma's Scrabble days were over, and she was confined to a nursing home. For many months, I looked at Scrabble boxes with selfish anger.

In April 2013, the boys and I went back to Iowa for a belated Easter celebration. With the dinner dishes done and adults wandering around at loose ends, I found

Mom's Scrabble box, dusted it off, and rallied together four players: my sister-in-law, my sister, my mom, and me. When those wooden letter tiles jiggled in the bag, they drew my three nieces to the table: six-, five-, and two-year-olds.

Our game in April was not about the biggest word or the most points. It was about a two-year-old counting and pulling tiles, a five-year-old dumping the rack as she rearranged tiles, and a six-year-old reading the word aloud that was to be played the next round. Suddenly it hit me . . . what incredible patience Grandma drew from a very deep well as her grandkids' small fingers rummaged through her Scrabble rack throughout the last forty years.

Grandma's ten fingers weren't present at the table that day in April, but seventy fingers from three generations were carrying on that Sunday afternoon tradition. Triple word score for forty-eight points, *HEAVEN*, with the *H* on a double letter score.

When Grandma passed away, Bill and I decided that the boys should go to the funeral. The visitation was Sunday afternoon and the funeral was on Monday.

When I got the news about Grandma, I waited twelve hours to tell my sons that she had died. It took that long to work out what to say to our then-eight- and six-year-old sons. Grandma had lived a very long time, and her body was worn out. We were going back to Iowa for Grandma's funeral – a celebration of her life. Grandma's soul was in heaven, but Grandma didn't need her body in heaven. The funeral was a way for people to say goodbye to Grandma's body. Grandma would look like she was sleeping in a box called a casket.

How did Grandma die? Grandma's kidneys failed. The kidneys are a major organ, and those organs need to work together. When one fails, they all begin to fail. Did it hurt? No, the doctors gave Grandma medicine so she wouldn't hurt. She died while she was sleeping – but only because her major organs were worn out. You can live without a leg like your other great-grandma did. A leg isn't a major organ. But kidneys, heart, and lungs, those are.

"What about a mandible, Mom?" Liam asked with a giggle. "I think that's somewhere on the head." Liam had been building up his anatomical vocabulary in a weekly human body workshop at school that spring.

At the funeral home, the flowers around Grandma's casket weren't funeral flowers. Mom said they had asked the florist for garden flowers. Three bouquets of summer's best, from roses and lilies to irises and daisies, were in perfect full bloom.

The visitation started quietly with just the immediate family before the doors opened to extended family and friends. At ninety-five years old, Grandma did not have many friends at the funeral. They were already waiting at the Scrabble board. Yet over two hundred people came to give their condolences – family and friends who had bloomed from one matriarch.

Grandma had taught school before she became a mother, long before she became a grandmother and a great-grandmother to forty-three grandchildren. At the visitation, I chatted with cousins that I had not seen in years, and I needed introductions to their children and significant others.

Will chose not to go up to see Grandma in the casket. By the end of the day, he was walking by the casket; still, he never approached it. Liam wanted to see Grandma. I was with him on the first visit when the young undertaker came over to talk to us. On bended knee, he pointed out Grandma's pink cheeks and immediately put one hand up above his own head and one down low. He explained to Liam that he had put blush on Grandma's face because when the heart stops pumping, blood stops circulating. After that thirty-second explanation, the undertaker held his hands side-by-side: the one that had been above his head was white while the one down low was very red. Liam was impressed.

Then, Liam reached out to touch Grandma's hand. My whispered "D" in "don't" was overshadowed by the undertaker's matter-of-fact "Sure, you can touch Grandma." So Liam touched her hand.

Another time at the casket, my aunt joined Liam. They chatted a bit, and then my aunt walked away. From ten feet away, I saw Liam's mouth say, "Are you *really* dead, Grandma?"

Later my aunt said that he had told her he thought he had seen Grandma's chest move like she was breathing. My aunt had confirmed that she wasn't alive, that she was with God.

"So it was like an optical illusion?" Liam asserted with some question.

Liam checked in at the casket throughout the day. I followed him up a few times and ultimately decided he was just curious and didn't need more explanation.

After the visitation, Liam confided in me some information for which I needed an oxygen mask to drop down from the heavens. "You know, Mom, I couldn't get Grandma's mouth open."

After I murmured, "Thank you, dear Lord," and *really* meaning it, the definition of *mandible* hit me. Mandible . . . the bottom jaw.

Once a teacher, always a teacher. Grandma, thanks for that one last lesson.

# The Gold Maple

———◆———

When we found our property here in New England, we loved that it was surrounded by maple trees. The first autumn, we filled five leaf bags and didn't even make a dent in the piles. We needed help raking. Now, every year, we have a four-hour show: a crew of five people with industrial leaf blowers, accompanied by a covered dump truck with an attached giant vacuum cleaner. It has an eighteen-inch-wide tubular mouth that sucks the leaves into the truck bed.

The second spring at our new house, we hired another company to remove some dead trees. As we pointed out specific ones to be removed, the arborist commented on our maples overall. "These are scrub maples. . . . They pop up and multiply like rabbits."

I stuck up for the maples and said they provided a thick, natural privacy fence. Still, I could tell he would've taken great satisfaction in cutting them all down.

That fall, we paid more attention to the leaves. They turned a dirty brown/yellow before they fell. Indeed, our maples weren't the vibrant beauties you think of when you hear the words "fall in New England."

Finally, eight years later, I decided we needed at least one true New England maple. At our local nursery, I asked for a gold sugar maple. The man cocked his head and said, "Which one do you want?"

He explained that there is a gold maple and a sugar maple. The gold maple leaves turn bright yellow in the fall. The sugar maple leaves turn splendid yellow, orange, and red. The other major difference is that gold maples take ten years to mature, and sugar maples take twenty-five years. Needing instant gratification, I chose the gold maple.

Before we planted the new tree, a few spindly maple trees had to come down. We called our tree removal company, and a man came out to give us an estimate. I pointed to the trees to be taken out, and he spray-painted a red *X* on each one. He looked at the root-bound ground and asked, "How are you going to dig a hole big enough for the root ball?"

I shrugged.

He offered to dig the hole with a stump grinder. He had a glint in his eye like a kid with a new toy.

A few days later, the arborist backed a trailer into our drive. On it was a big machine with the word *Vermeer* across the side. That company is headquartered in Pella, Iowa! For years, we had driven by the sprawling equipment manufacturing plant on the way to our friends' house. I knew Vermeer only as a company that had told me I was on the right road. Now, sitting in my drive was a stump grinder from that very company! Believing that small things point to good karma, I knew planting this tree would be a successful endeavor.

I directed where the tree was to stand, and the men maneuvered the grinder into place. The mechanism dropped to the ground and spun wide and deep enough for the root ball. It spat out rocks and broke through thick tree roots, creating a nest for the new tree's baby roots. It was obvious that the arborist loved his job by the way his face lit up as the machine did the work. Having a big enough hole, he and his assistant cut off the gunnysack from around the root ball and dropped the tree into place. They filled in the dirt, making sure the tree stood up straight.

"Now you get the hard part of keeping it alive! You see where I left a six-inch-deep trench around the tree? Fill it with water twice a day until mid-October." It was June.

Faithfully, I filled the trench with two gallons of water morning and night. I dug out the trench when too much dirt washed in after heavy rains. When we went on vacation for a week, I left specific watering instructions for our neighbors who were watering flower beds while we were away. I showed our sons, Will and Liam, how to gradually pour water in the moat and let it seep into the ground a bit, rather than creating a dam burst with a torrential pour.

In the fall, the leaves turned gold and fell, just as New England maple leaves should. Bill told the snowplow guy not to knock it over when he plowed at 2 a.m. Come spring, it budded and new leaves sprang forth. On hot days, when the leaves drooped, I set up a sprinkler and let a small arch of water fall on and around the gold maple for an hour.

Now, every time I come home from my daily drives, I park right in front of it and give it the once-over. Every time I park, a little checkup. Three or four times a day.

One afternoon, I came home and looked at the tree, and it occurred to me, *I want to be that tree. I want a foundation of space carved out for me and a trench with a reservoir of nutrients for mind, body, and soul. Who but me will tend to all of this? To observe a daily habit of care. To check that I'm not wilting.*

I think back to when I was going through breast cancer treatment and when my doctor told me that my first priority was myself. Really, that should always be the case. How else do we expect to take care of others if we aren't taking the very best care of ourselves? Our needs change day to day, week to week. We should check in frequently, making it a habit as natural as brushing our teeth or taking a shower. What we need doesn't necessarily come knocking at our door. Rather, if we purposely think about our needs, then we can be attentive to fulfilling them.

A fall walk in the woods when the leaves are lit with color. Dancing to "I Feel Good" playing loudly in the kitchen. A fifteen-minute conversation with a friend every day. A meal in a restaurant that doesn't serve chicken fingers and grilled cheese. Sleep. FaceTiming with Mom and Dad. Drinking more water. Taking a half hour to sit down and eat lunch. Stirring a pot of risotto for a half hour. Digging in the warming spring ground and planting young seedling flowers.

I'm the only one who knows what I need – if I take the time to give myself the same occasional once-over as I do that tree. A certain calm comes from deep within me when I care for myself as I do for the people in my life – and for one gold maple with a moat to receive daily nutrients.

# Turkeys and Love

Ahhhh, Thanksgiving morn. I feel a telepathic scuttle every year when my alarm goes off early that morning. Turkey energy is running through kitchens all across the country. Houses are quiet but for the one person carrying the load of the day: preparing the turkey.

In our house, I'm the director, and Bill does the hands-on lifting, cleaning, rubbing, and carving. We had a special guest of honor a couple of years ago: our turkey had lived a charmed life roaming on a small farm west of Boston. The Sunday before that Thanksgiving, Bill drove to the distribution point to collect our gobbler.

My name wasn't on the typed list, but the farmer remembered talking to me. She asked, "What size did Linda order?"

Bill hadn't a clue about the weight of turkeys. "Probably a medium."

So on that day, our turkey grew from 14-16 pounds to 17-20 pounds for four people. There were actually six of us, but I was pretty sure Will and Liam wouldn't try the turkey. The poem "Point of View" by Shel Silverstein was read by one of the students at an all-school Thanksgiving meeting that previous Monday. Many of us chuckled at it. However, my son Will used it to justify exactly why mac 'n' cheese is a perfectly good Thanksgiving entrée.

All week I had been visualizing that beautifully roasted, domed bird. Bill had been giving it cold baths daily, per the farmer's direction, then covering it with a wet towel and foil, and returning it to the fridge. I had been studying the many options of preparation: brining, buttering, herbing, or simply shoving it into a 350-degree oven. Since we were having an evening feast, I decided to brine it for the day in kosher salt in a sinkful of ice water.

At 6:30 that morning, Bill carried the turkey up from the basement fridge and uncovered it as I gave directions. "I think it should go breast down so that the meat is fully submerged in the brine."

We started filling the sink with water and ice. Bill placed the turkey into the prep sink. I restated, "No, it needs to go breast down."

Looking at me as if I had two heads, Bill said, "It *is* breast down. It's been this way all week."

Thus we entered a peculiar quiet state of "I'm right". . . "No, I'm right." But I knew I was right. As sure as I could tell the pungent difference between cow manure and pig shit, I was right. At this impasse, I couldn't speak. Both of us stared at the tail, the elbow of the wing – and yes, the backbone – for several seconds. Finally, I broke the silence. "Bill, do you really think this is the breast?"

Pause. Sigh. "No. . . . Now I don't."

Our once wide DD breasted turkey was now a wide BB. Flat-chested. Condensed. Flat as a pancake. She had been lying comatose on her breasts for four days.

# Lumps of Sugar

At the age of 80, my mother-in-law, June, was no longer able to live independently in her own house. While Bill had lived an ocean away, his sister, Anne, had lived next door to her mum. She and her husband had the ominous task of emptying and selling the house. Now, when we visit England, we find a place to rent – sometimes a house, sometimes in a hotel. Anne hates that she can't accommodate our family of four in her home; we hate that she had the responsibility of moving their mum from her home.

For our 2017 Christmas visit to England, we stayed in a hotel where my mornings started with dark coffee at the hotel's restaurant, the Rump & Wade. Being the early riser in our family, each night before I went to bed I laid out my clothes and packed a book and a journal for my morning excursion.

We stayed in Stevenage at the Cromwell Hotel, named after Oliver Cromwell. The hotel was not so named because this political leader lived there in the early to mid-1600s, but rather that John Thurloe, his secretary, owned the building, then a farmhouse. I interpret *secretary* to be like a cabinet member. Thurloe was Cromwell's head of intelligence. It seemed strange to me that I awoke every morning to Cromwell's portrait on the wall of Thurloe's home. I wrote that off to modern-day marketing.

The Rump & Wade is the bar and restaurant connected by a long hallway to the Cromwell. We Malcolms had a little giggle at the name. During the English Civil War in the mid-1600s, Cromwell led the English Parliament after the death of Charles I. Within a government torn apart by war, Cromwell led the remnant group that remained, the *rump*.

As for Wade, well, honestly, the origins of Rump held a bigger fascination to me than Wade. Perhaps it refers to George Wade, who was born in the generation following Cromwell and served in four wars throughout his lifetime. Just an educated guess at that one, based on a little poking around at the history of *wade* in England. Naturally, most references were to walking through shallow water. I would hope that the name Rump & Wade has a deeper meaning than that.

The Cromwell is fitted out with beautiful dark wood paneling, and the long hallway to the Rump & Wade is painted Caribbean blue. It opens into a brightly lit brasserie with a bar and tables for breakfast in the morning or lounging in the evening. The connected restaurant seating is reserved for more formal lunches and dinners. A small table near the window was my morning retreat.

Every morning, the tables were fully set, including a little pitcher of milk for English breakfast tea and a bowl of sugar cubes. My table was set for breakfast, but I wanted *elevenses*: coffee, not tea. It's customary to take a short break and have coffee or tea around 11:00 in the morning, with a little something to go with it, like a biscuit (cookie) or bun (sweet roll). I was asking for elevenses at sevenses.

However, coffee was readily available in the hotel restaurant with freshly brewed American-style pots waiting on the sidelines next to the bar. When the waitress served coffee to me the first day, I asked for cream. She took my request in stride and brought a small pitcher of cream to the table. I didn't bother asking for sweetener instead of sugar. I had sent the bar into a bit of a shuffle asking for sweetener the night before. It would be a sugar-filled week with two lumps in each cup of coffee.

As I grew up on a farm in rural northeastern Iowa, lumps of sugar in sweet little bowls were not prolific in my childhood. Lumps of sugar were used infrequently and never in the context of a fresh linen-covered breakfast table. My uncle occasionally took my sister and me horseback riding, and after riding, we would feed the horses lumps of white sugar from our flat, outstretched hands, flat like a table so the horses' lips would tickle them and their teeth wouldn't nibble them. I can't help but think these little lumps are horse treats served up as posh on the English table. Don't get me wrong; we have sugar cubes in the States, too – but not at the pub, burger joint, or our other kid-friendly haunts.

Lumps of sugar slow the consumption of coffee. Not once in England did I pour coffee into a travel mug with a dash of sweetener and a splash of half-and-half to gulp on the way to somewhere. It was a nice change of pace. When I ordered coffee the first morning at the Rump

& Wade, I smiled and put on my best American accent to ask for a little pot of cream to go with it. My smile was an apologetic "I'm-so-sorry-I'm-an-American-drinking-coffee-at-7-a.m.-asking-for-cream."

However, the first six days, the same waitress was there every morning, and she knew my routine by day three. Then on day seven, a new waitress – and complete confusion.

"You can just help yourself to coffee over by the bar," she replied as I wandered around with an empty coffee cup.

"Oh, I'm so sorry. I didn't realize it was self-service!" Why hadn't the day one through six waitress said something?

"Oh, it's not, but I assumed since you were right there . . ."

"May I have a little bit of cream, too, please?" I asked as she poured the coffee into the cup in my hand.

"If we have any" was her reply as she walked behind the bar. She found the cream. "How much do you want?" She was going to glug the cream into my cup directly from the gallon jug. Yes, in England, gallons of cream.

I couldn't say tablespoon – I think that's American – yet I wanted more than an English teaspoon. "Just a little splash," I decided. The translation would have been easier had she just poured a little in a pot for me.

I took my cup back to the table and found no sugar bowl. I borrowed the one from the next table. And this being the seventh day, I let the thought fully develop: How many other people's fingers had reached into this sugar bowl to grab a lump of sugar? There were neither sugar tongs nor a spoon in the sugar bowl. I was sure that many people, just like me, had reached in for a lump or two with their fingers. I saw rows of sugar bowls full and stacked up behind the bar. This was not a disposable set of cubes. The bowl was moved from table to table and refilled as needed. I wondered how often they were cleaned.

Conflicting thoughts between packeted sweeteners and bowls of sugar cubes bounced around in my brain. How many trees do we chop down in order to individually package truckloads of quarter teaspoons of sugar? And the accompanying three different sweeteners in the "sugar bowl"? How many kids, including my own, create wasteful restaurant games out of these packets? The stateside health department's intolerance of germs seems to have swung the sugar pendulum ridiculously far from simply serving sugar cubes. Or is it easier for restaurants to receive shipments of tiny packets than lumps of sugar? I was in full sugar spin.

The lunacy over sugar ended when, after dropping two cubes of sugar into my morning coffee, I opened my journal to write. The memory of horse lips tickling my palms forty years ago reminded me of swimming with stingrays, for the underside of a stingray ranks number one as the softest object I've ever touched — second only to those horse lips taking sugar cubes off of my ten-year-old hand. Yes, sugar cubes over Christmas brought back a memory that pushed velvety horse lips to second, outranking the silkiness of my sons' cheeks as babies.

# A 25-Year-Old Piece of Oak

My 1992 living room table sails on the floor of my New England 1880 dining room. I push the table against the east wall, and a few days later it has slid down the wave toward the matching china closet. It doesn't sail symmetrically. One leg is a little closer to the opposite wall – the good leg. The leg across from it on the width twists as if it's fighting the movement. I lift the tabletop up and pop the leg back into place, a bit like a chiropractic adjustment on old bones. As with marbles and pens that are dropped on the floor, the table is pulled toward the low side of the dining room. I see this and hope that our 140-year-old house has finally settled. With any more listing, I envision the original 1880 structure detaching from the circa 1970 addition.

Bill and I bought the oak table, six chairs, and a china hutch with money we received as gifts when we were married in 1992. Two chairs are in the garage waiting for a ride to a woodworker to rejuvenate them. Two leaves stand in the basement at the ready to convert the six-foot-long table to a nine-foot-long table. The matching china hutch holds many of the goblets we also received as wedding gifts. When a fast-paced walk through the dining room makes the crystal clink as if a real toast were underway, I know it's time to pull the goblets away from the hutch's mirrored back. They, too, are subject to the gravitational pull of the wall opposite the table.

Setting the table when we have company takes more than putting place settings around the perimeter of the rectangular slab. Ideally, this is a two-person job. Standing near the wall, Bill and I lift the end of the table, pull it toward the wall, then straighten the legs before setting it down. Then we move to the other end of the table, lift it again, and straighten those legs. Finally, I run my hand along the top back of each of the chairs and, with my fingernails, push in the sharp points of the wood nails that poke out. Otherwise, they would scratch or jab our guests.

The tabletop shows its age. The marks from hot bowls and the peeling dry wood remind me of all the people who have sat at or walked around this table. I think when Bill sees the same imperfections, the table registers as an asset that we haven't taken care of very well. For his sake, I always keep a tablecloth on it, and if I want to change it for company, I do it quickly and discreetly.

The biggest culprit of that ragged tabletop is most likely our curry open house nights some sixteen years ago. With many Brits and cooks in our social circle, we started an annual tradition in the dead of winter. Each February we put the word out: bring an Indian dish to share, and the Malcolms will provide India pale ale (IPA) beer. Indian food only. No exceptions. The fully extended 108-inch dining room table was filled with mouthwatering Indian dishes from fifteen different families. As the party grew in size the third year, I knew we would be short on serving spoons. I sent out an email asking everyone to bring serving utensils. One couple, not sure exactly what I was looking for, brought their entire utensil drawer. I think we used ice cream scoops to serve basmati rice that evening.

Couples, a couple of couples, and a few couples have sat down to dinner at this table. Family from Iowa. Family from England. Local friends. Illinois friends. Massachusetts friends. Friends who traveled great distances to "snack around the Malcolm table." Breakfasts, lunches, and dinners. Science and social studies projects. Uncountable nights and days, that tabletop has gathered people together.

At a Christmas cookie swap I hosted one year, only two invitees were able to come. Still, it was an evening filled with great conversation and laughter. As I reflect on this scene, the people I "see" outnumber the guests who were there. My friends from Rockford, Illinois, who gave us the cork wreath decorated in gold for the holidays that hangs above the table at Christmastime; my dad, who, when I was a teen, brought back a big round platter for me from California, which displays a multitude of homemade cookies; my grandma, whose tablecloth graces the table; my mom, who gave me the gold stand that elevates five small plates of cookies; my college roommate, whose grandmother gave me the recipe for thumbprint cookies; and my sister-in-law, who gave me the sugar cookie recipe.

The resplendency of that Christmas table confirmed for me that although its joints are loose, the solid wood should carry us through another twenty-five years.

# Getting to Iowa: Christmas 2015

We had a Goliath-sized journey to Iowa and back for Christmas 2015. That year, the plan was to wake up in our house Christmas Day, a Friday morning, then spend the weekend relaxing at home before flying to Iowa on Monday. On December 22$^{nd}$, at the end of the school day, Liam said excitedly, "Tomorrow we fly to Iowa, right?" No. I reviewed the schedule with him.

Hearing our conversation in the background, Will said, "But I've been waiting for a week already!" The 18$^{th}$ had been the last day of school for him. "But we are only going to be there for FIVE DAYS! That's not long enough!"

Sunday evening, we received an email telling us that our 2:00 p.m. flight on Monday had been canceled and rebooked to 4:13 p.m. the same day. Snowstorm Goliath was wreaking havoc across the country, with two feet of snow in the Midwest. Over 1,600 flights into Chicago had been canceled.

In the airport lounge Monday afternoon, we watched the screen for hours. Finally, the 4:13 p.m. flight was canceled, and no flight information for the next day was available. "I am not leaving this airport! I want to see my cousins in Iowa!" Will complained.

After eating at Legal Sea Foods in the terminal, we checked with the ticket agent. No room on Tuesday's flights, but surely they would add more flights to accommodate passengers. "Check after midnight," we were told. We traveled home to sleep in our own beds.

*Travail is the derivation of travel. To travail means to engage in painful and laborious effort, as does a woman in labor.*

At 6:00 a.m. on Tuesday, I spent an hour on the phone waiting and reviewing our options. No flights to Chicago. No flights to Cedar Rapids, Dubuque, or Des Moines. We couldn't fly to Iowa until Wednesday. "What about Minneapolis? Can you get us to Minneapolis?"

Yes. A 2:30 p.m. flight on Tuesday would get us there in the early evening.

I scampered to rebook the car rental – putting my fingers in my ears and singing "la-la-la" to drown out the price of picking up a car in one city and returning it in another.

At the airport Tuesday afternoon, we checked in again and arrived at the gate to see that the flight had been delayed to 5:00 p.m.

"What?" Will moaned.

Equipment problems. The plane is in the hangar. No, wait! It's on the way over! Oops, wrong plane . . . it's still in the hangar. We decided to have a late lunch – at Legal Sea Foods, in a different terminal from where we had eaten the day before.

Back at the gate, we got wind of unofficial news. "We don't have confidence in this plane flying today."

Will: "I AM NOT LEAVING THIS AIRPORT!"

*Travail's origin from Middle English is via Old French from Medieval Latin. Trepalium: an instrument of torture. Tre = three. Pallium = stake. To impale yourself on three stakes.*

Around 7:00 p.m. on Tuesday, it was confirmed that the plane was grounded, but a plane arriving from Minneapolis at 8:30 p.m. was going to head back with us on board at 9:30 p.m. We had dinner at Legal Sea Foods. Again. I booked a hotel in Minneapolis for our midnight arrival. That became a 2:00 a.m. Wednesday arrival after a very late 11:00 p.m. departure from Boston on Tuesday.

On the umpteenth call to Mom and Dad, Dad said, "I don't know about these Christmas plans!" Gotta love him. He would've liked us there the first of December.

This journey unfolded like a scene from *Home Alone* or *Planes, Trains and Automobiles*. We were powerless, given immovable obstacles and left with the challenge of overcoming them. Powerless children felt this most acutely.

Facing long drives, I used to tell the kids that to get to the good stuff, sometimes you have to do things that aren't pleasant – but worth it for what's at the other end. For if we hadn't had Goliath, we wouldn't have had snow, and snow was the number one thing on the wish list for Christmas in Iowa. Once we returned to Massachusetts, Will acknowledged the necessity of Goliath. Without it, there would have been no tobogganing behind the four-wheel ATV. When I took the driver's seat and control of the throttle, my nine-year-old nephew urged, "Show us how much farm girl you have left in you, Aunt Linda!" Through the wide-open cornstalk-stubbled field, I gunned the gas and left him sliding off the back of the toboggan as the other three kids held on in fits of giggles. Grinning nonstop, I felt gleeful power in controlling the speed and direction of that four-wheeler.

*Travel: a journey taken for enjoyment and relaxation with friends and family.*

# The Crash of the Christmas Tree

A day after I had nearly finished decorating the Christmas tree of 2016, the thing went over. I hadn't put any hand-painted glass balls on it. I lost only two ornaments. One was a 3D glass lace heart. Twenty-five years old. The anger over the flipping tree overshadowed any soppy nostalgia over the broken glass scattered on the carpet and across the hardwood floor.

We have no pets. No one was near the tree. Will and Liam were upstairs in their bedrooms. I was in the kitchen when I heard it go, and Bill was at work. The culprit of the crash? We'd bought a crooked tree. The trunk was straight as an arrow in the tree stand. The day we put it up, I did notice the top leaning a bit forward but didn't think it was a big deal. Not big enough to send the engineer back under there. However, I should have sent the engineer in for a design change before it heaved over.

That evening, after much tweaking, Bill and I decided that it was well and truly crooked, and that the best option was to turn it so it leaned into the corner. The back of the tree became the front. The back, which had been facing the window and which no one in the house would see. There those tacky ornaments hung, the ones of which I'm not quite sure of their origin – but I feel the need to keep them. It took a full twenty-four hours for me to step up to the tree to redecorate it. I mulled over the idea of leaving it as it was. However, Aunt Ruth's crocheted string of beads that had been roped like garland back and forth on the true front were just barely showing on one side of the tree. Sheer evidence of an "oops."

I threw a picture of the fallen tree onto Facebook. That post became a support group for those of us who'd had this most unfortunate experience. Two people had lost one the weekend before ours went over. One mom's went over three times in one day — once landing on her littlest boy! She has four boys. He wasn't injured, probably pretty used to being on the bottom of a pile.

The Christmas tree. What a lovely tradition in my Norman Rockwell frame of mind. And to me, the decorating is as big a part of tradition as gazing googly-eyed at the completed twinkly tree. Despite my wish for "a Christmas tree tradition," this year's putting-up-the-tree has pushed me to rethink what should be involved in this tradition. What should this tradition look like for my family? For a multitude of reasons, I realize I have been defining this step-by-step, beginning to end in my mind, and hoping the implementation will follow smoothly when adding a man, a young boy, and a male teenager to the mix. Seriously, what the hell am I thinking?

I'll tell you.

When my sons have families of their own, I want them to be involved in the making of traditions and to know that there is value in it — for themselves and for their loved ones. Traditions take more than one person implementing a plan. It starts there but depends on buy-in, although I now realize there are various degrees of buy-in.

Bill is allergic to the poke of the pine needles and the sap and the bark. So to put the tree up the first time – and the second time – he hauled out his leather gloves to wrestle with the heavy end. To place ornaments on what must be to Bill a giant poisonous pincushion, he would be wearing leather gloves for hours, pretending to enjoy it for me.

When the thing went over, only the boys were home with me. I called Will down to help me pull it upright. He didn't want to touch it. He's not keen on the prickly needles, yet he gingerly picked up the top while I reached in barehanded and hugged the tree to my chest to get it to stand at attention. He balanced it while I examined the tree stand. At that point, we had not yet determined it was a crooked tree. All we could do was lean it into a corner and shove a large hardback book of *The Complete Adventures of Curious George* under one side of the tree stand so it wouldn't topple again. Then we waited for Bill to get home. My thoughts were dark as I struggled unsuccessfully to fix it. I would never be able to do this on my own. If Bill kicks off before me, there goes my tree stabilizer.

With the repair round of decorating looming, I reflected on the first round. I had removed special metal ornaments from their boxes so that when the boys helped decorate, they didn't need to mess with unpacking ornaments, which is my least favorite part of decorating. As I prepped for family tree trimming, Bill and Will stayed in the kitchen. They were within sight of the tree, but their eyes were cast firmly downward toward projects on the kitchen counter, avoiding decorating the tree. Liam hung perhaps two or three ornaments on the tree before he sat down on a chair three feet away from me. With his feet up, he chatted away as I decorated. I invited him to join in again.

Looking out of the corner of his eye with a devilish self-protecting smile, Liam said, "I'm providing charisma to the tree decorating!" Liam also hates anything poky, let alone sappy and sticky.

I'll be damned. I'm the only one who loves muscling the tree without gloves and poking lights into the interior branches so the whole thing glows. I'm the only one who knows where each ornament came from and who wants those memories to be part of the ornament-hanging experience. I'm the only one who enjoys the pushback of the tree as I lean into it while standing on a step stool to put the star on top.

I'm not saying the three wise men in my house don't enjoy the memories, but perhaps not all in one sitting. Maybe occasionally, walking by the tree, they see an ornament that reminds them of the drive to South Dakota with their aunt, two cousins, Grandpa and Grandma, and no electronics. They are happy with one memory at a time. As for me, I need full memory immersion for my putting-up-the-tree experience to be complete.

Maybe after the tree is up, some other traditions will take hold. It must be told that the string of beads represents more than Aunt Ruth, but also Will and Liam's great-grandma Mills and her spunky sisters: Aunt Dorothy, the eldest and calmest; Aunt Hazel, the baby and the most mischievous; Aunt Betty, the snoopy one who opened closed doors when visiting her sisters; and Aunt Ruth, the round one and the ally to their great-grandma Mills. Those two would share an eyeball roll as Aunt Ruth would say, "Lock the doors. Betty is on her way over." That's the story that spins when I string those beads back and forth across the tree.

Down to its skinniest form, what is my expectation of setting up this dead tree in my house? It must be real – dead but real. It must have ornaments that bring back memories. It must have a star. It must have at least six hundred white lights. It must have candy canes. It must be lit from sunup to sundown. Ideally, it will be lit when the kids come down in the morning and still lit as they go off to bed.

And what are my basic needs during the setting up of the tree? Help lodging it into the tree base and turning it until I detect the front of the tree. Help picking it up if it falls over. And a little bit of charisma from Liam would be mighty helpful in keeping me company while on task.

# The Rotund Tree's Slow Evolution

I write this while sitting next to our 2017 lit Christmas tree. It's not decorated, just lit. The tree is a round-as-it-is-tall Fraser fir.

While picking this tree out, we Malcolms stuck close to our yearly patter of this outing. It is known as chore or tradition, depending on which Malcolm you ask.

Scene One, I point to the perfect tree. Then Bill raises his arm straight up to prove he is unable to touch the top bough, saying, "This one is too tall for our living room." Before resigning to that opinion, I drop my head to the trunk to see how much we can cut off. I decide that's too much of a gamble and concede that we should not pay for an extra two feet when that's how much needs to be chopped off the bottom before it goes into the house.

Scene Two, we move on to the neighboring tree, beginning the search for one with the same shape as that first tree.

Scene Three, many minutes later, we finally achieve a four-way consensus on the perfect round, just-the-right-height tree.

On this trip, it took the tree salesman longer to explain the difference between a fir and a spruce than it did for us to find the tree. Our rotund tree was the second tree we looked at, only three trees down from the too-big ten-footer.

We were at a new Christmas tree lot that had elves deliver the tree to our house via a sleigh on wheels. Dressed in elf costumes, they pulled it behind their work truck that they use in their irrigation business during the three other New England seasons. The elves even brought the tree inside and set it up in our tree stand. I thought this experience would be a welcome change for my Chief Tree-Putting-Up Elf, Bill. With our previous year's crash, Bill had spent more time under the tree straightening it than watching the twinkling lights from afar. It was a welcome break to let two professional elves take care of this job.

While the tree was still wrapped in netting, I fed it two tablespoons of sugar in warm water per the elves' direction. The elves told us to leave it for about an hour before we cut the netting off and released the branches. During that time, Bill noticed it was slightly askew, so he, Will, and I adjusted the angle of the trunk just a little bit, looking for 90-degree angles between trunk and floor from all vantage points. Finally, I cut the netting off, and the branches shyly released. When I went to bed, they were still reaching for the ceiling.

At first sight of the tree the next morning, I gasped, for many reasons. There's the tree! Yay, we have a tree! It's so beautiful! Then . . . oh my goodness, how did it get so wide? How will I drag it out of here in January when it's now twice as wide as the back door? The tree is nearly hugging the love seat!

Sidebar: I have visual perspective issues. Salmon fillets double in size from the fish counter to my kitchen counter. Soup recipes calling for ten cups of stock surely would be better if doubled. Hanging a picture on the wall usually ends in scratches on the paint because I can't accurately visualize the placement of the hook on the back of the photo frame relative to the nail on the wall. For me to get a golf ball into the hole in the green? Forget about it.

So it goes with this tree. However, now that I've moved the computer hutch over twelve inches and the love seat back two feet, this oversized tree is magnificent. The green breadth of the tree has stolen the living room focal point away from the wide-screen TV.

Last night, I found the small tub of white tree lights and pushed the strings into the depths of the branches toward the trunk. Eight strings later, I had hardly made a visible glow. I had two brand-new strings of colored lights, so I added those to the mix. This could work, yet I saw plenty of room for more twinkle. Once the wattage was at an acceptable level, I would start adding the decorations. From past experience, I know it makes the most sense to be happy with the lighting before putting ornaments on the tree.

Every year, I get a bit better at accepting the fact that I do not, cannot, shall not put the tree up in one day, as I did when I was in my twenties. Now there are more lights to buy, twenty-five years of accumulated ornaments to hang, and four schedules to coordinate. I might get twenty ornaments hung on a Wednesday, none the next day, five on Friday, and finish over the weekend.

Acknowledging this makes tree trimming much more enjoyable than fretting over the slowness of the process. The rides to and from basketball, gymnastics, scouts, trumpet lessons, drum lessons, STEM classes — not to mention the daily school drop-off and pickup — make for intermittent decorating. Fact.

I decided that I would appreciate the few minutes it took to put on that year's new baubles from Maine, Kennedy Space Center, Vermont, Boston, and Iowa. And I will be grateful for the friends and our family who have woven memories with us throughout the year.

We have a lovely pudgy Fraser fir from which to hang many years' worth of commemorations, celebrations, and reminiscences.

# Memories in the Hall

As the New Year of 2018 started, I looked around me to see that much in our house reflects the past. The comfort of familiar nostalgia just may be beginning to bog me down. The longest hallway in our house reaches from the doorway to the kitchen near the back door and runs the length of the mudroom and the laundry room. It's eighteen feet long and filled with photos in black and white frames of our family, both Bill's side and mine.

Since 2012, when we renovated the house and created this hallway, the photos haven't changed too much. With no family living near us, I wanted a hallway filled with family photos to remind our sons, Will and Liam, of their connections to their people who are hundreds of miles east and west of Massachusetts. Consequently, there are only three rows of photos, and the bottom row is at the height of a seven-year-old. That's how old our younger son, Liam, was when I put up the photos. Walking through the hall one day, Will asked, "These are so old. Why don't you put newer pictures up?"

The answer is not so much that I don't have space. There is plenty of room to make another row above the current grouping, particularly since the boys are seven years taller now. Most of these photos are touchpoints in the past, marking good times with family in Iowa and England throughout the boys' childhood. Plus pictures of their great-grandparents, who hold such a big space in my memory that I wanted the boys to at least know the faces of their grandparents' stories. The boys have sufficient personal memories now to have a clear feeling of place in a family that isn't down the street or in the next town over.

I wonder who lingers in this hallway all that much? It's a straight shot from the upstairs bedrooms to the bottom of the stairs, through the office and down this hall to the back door. It's heavily trafficked, but few pause in this thoroughfare.

For Christmas 2017, Bill's sister gave us a framed black-and-white photo of our nephew playing guitar on stage. It's in a 10"x10" black 3D frame. I saw the photo on their living room wall when we arrived a couple of days before Christmas. I was going to ask her for a copy of it, and then there it was under the tree. If ever there was a photo that summed up a beautiful journey from child to adult, this was it. He's looking down intensely at his guitar as he's playing. In black and white, his t-shirt is gray and his black leather vest pops with stagelike presence. There is true grit in the photo. He's not looking outward to the world or to his parents for guidance; he's truly come into his own passion, and his confidence exudes from the photo. That photo had to find a place on the wall. So a photo of him as a young teen with guitar in hand came off the wall.

In a vein of honesty, since this photo was a gift, it was easier to replace the old with the new. To look through photos to find more current ones to blow up and frame? That's a rabbit hole I could fall into for weeks. I would pull up the most current on my iPhone, do a small scroll back through fall, hit summer in Iowa, and find twenty photos by the time I reached the beginning of last year. And my inclination would be to keep going. Ah, boundaries . . . I could set the limit of going only to the beginning of the previous year, yet that would eliminate the Christmas in the previous year where I see so many adorable photos at the tiniest flick of my fingertip. I'm already overwhelmed. I'm not confident that I could abide by such time constraints.

However, it's doable. If the kids are noticing these aging framed photos, then the prints inside need a redo. They've seen them often enough for the moment to have become a memory. Will sitting on a rock with my dad in Marblehead, Massachusetts, with the ocean behind them. Will standing next to my mom in the butterfly exhibit at the Museum of Science in Boston. In that picture, the top of his head is at her waist. Today, Will is slightly taller than Grandma. These photos are from Grandpa and Grandma's first trip out to see us. And from that same trip, a photo of Liam pulling a pen out of a pocket in Grandpa's striped bib overalls, the same type of bibs he wears every day in Iowa. Liam doesn't need to be reminded of that pen, for over the last ten years, he and Grandpa have regularly held contests of who-can-hold-the-pencil-under-his-nose-the-longest on Skype. Yes, those photos can come down.

I'm moving in the direction of updating, and I think I know how to do it: the same way Mom does. I'll put the new photos in and leave the old photos behind the new ones in the frame.

# Hiking in the Berkshires

In January 2018, I went away for a long weekend, a solo writing retreat from Friday through Tuesday. Late Sunday morning, my reward for four hours of early morning work was a snowy hike. Around 11 a.m., I pulled on my boots and briefly looked at a trail map of Beartown State Forest, near where I was staying in South Lee, Massachusetts. On the map, I found a short loop trail around Benedict Pond, near the entrance to the park.

The bubbling anxiety of walking by myself was making me grumpy as I drove three miles on a narrow back road to get to the park entrance. I regularly walk in a state park near our house; more often than not, I go by myself and take the same route every time. For most of that local walk, I stay on the main paved trail where, time and again, I see many of the same runners, dog walkers, women, and men. I'm comfortable there on the forty-five-minute loop I make through the woods. However, I've absorbed fears that are illogical, and this place was new to me. Should I be hiking this trail alone?

I ponder my recent reading of *The Year of Living Danishly: Uncovering the Secrets of the World's Happiest Country*. The English author, Helen Russell, and her husband moved to Jutland, Denmark, so he could take a year-long assignment at LEGO's headquarters. She made it her mission to research why Danes were so happy, despite paying high taxes and living through cold, dark winters.

Russell found that high on the list of factors affecting their happiness is trust. As much as our American culture relies on lawsuits, Danes rely on trust. They trust the government to provide services with tax money. They leave babies in their strollers outside coffee shops while having lunch. They have a high degree of trust in people, which is unfathomable to many Americans. They trust *strangers*.

I want to have trust in my immediate world around me. I want to believe that people who cross my path are good. I want to see the world from the perspective that everyone is making the best decision they are capable of at any given time. Yet, what I had done with this whole walking-alone thing was sling words of fear into a bag and fling it over my shoulder to take with me on this winter wonderland walk. My mood grayed to match the winter sky.

When I pulled into the snowy parking lot, I saw four other cars already parked. Trying to shake my anxiousness, I thought, *This is good! There are other people here!* And then my self-talk flicked in the other direction. *But are they* good *people?*

Cussing to myself at this ridiculousness, I leaned against the van and pulled on snow-gripping Yaktrax over the bottoms of my boots. At the trailhead, I saw that the sign for Benedict Pond Road was pointing in either direction, so I knew I was on the loop trail. The path looked straight for about 200 yards before it bent slightly to the right. It was a narrow, snowy version of Highway 20, that straight, flat paved road that runs from border to border across Iowa. Only the path ahead of me was on a twenty-degree incline.

I heard a stream rushing to my right before I even started on the upward hike. I went 20 feet off trail to see the water up close. Half the width of the 20-foot-wide stream was still iced over, but the flowing water had hollowed out ice under the surface. In some places, there was a foot of open air between the inch-thick surface ice and the water running underneath it, leaving spectacular frozen formations. I soaked up the scene for a few minutes and then returned to the path. I felt happier about being alone.

*Hiking* is as broad a term as *beach*. When we have visitors and they want to go to the beach, I feel like handing them a questionnaire: Big surfing waves or wide tidal beach? Straight sandy beach or rocky bay? Lots of people or lots of space? Surfing or wading? Shell or sea glass seeking?

With hiking, I don't mind going up hills, as long as there is a little reprieve with a flat path or downhill after the uphill. I like going on steep hikes if I'm climbing up rocks, scrambling over tree roots, and grabbing onto trees to make my way. However, an endless walk on a 20-degree incline to the heavens was not my cup of tea.

Huffing and puffing, I kept going, visualizing the map that indicated the pond would be just around the next bend, but only another upward slant was around each bend. Finally, an hour into the walk, I came to a sign marked "Beebe Trail," a trail that I had seen signposted near the trailhead where I had started. I decided to give up on the pond loop trail as I knew Beebe Trail would loop around and come back out on the main road I'd been climbing. I noticed that the anxiety and shallow breathing I had experienced at the trailhead had now been replaced with deep, heavy breathing as I tackled the hill.

On Beebe Trail, I was only a few yards in when I headed up a steeper incline and found my left foot wouldn't hold on the snow and ice. Wondering if this steeper trail was such a good idea, I looked down to see that the Yaktrax on my left foot was missing. It had silently fallen off somewhere along the way. I wasn't going up Beebe Trail. I was going to backtrack the way I came to find my brand-new snow gripper. A half mile down the trail, I saw the curled-up piece of rubber and metal springs in the distance. I scooped it up and leaned against a tree to put it back on. I pulled the rubber fronts high over the toes of both boots, hoping that would keep them from falling off again.

With only fifteen minutes left in my hike down, I heard people and dogs behind me. At first glance, I saw the people had poles, so I thought they were cross-country skiing, but they weren't gliding. They were hikers decked out with spiky versions of my snow grippers on their feet, backpacks filled with water, and hiking poles. We exchanged hellos as we fell into step. I asked one of the men if he was familiar with Benedict Pond as that was where I thought I had been heading.

He thought a minute, then told me that the pond was near the main entrance, about eight miles away. Lost in thought over the idea of hiking alone, I had neglected to notice that the main entrance was not where I had entered the park. I was on Benedict Pond *Road*, not Benedict Pond *Loop Trail*.

I could tell by their chatting back and forth that these hikers, four men and two women, knew one another pretty well. I asked the same man if the group hiked together often. In fact, he told me, they hiked every Monday and Thursday year round. Starting in 1993, a group of retired men had decided to hike together on Mondays; they had originally dubbed themselves the "Monday Mountain Hiking Boys." Literally, an old boys' club, which now included women in the mix. The hiking group's founder was one of the founders of Kay Bee Toys – a Kaufman Brother who lived in Pittsfield. Every week, they hiked a different mountain in the Berkshires and enjoyed it so much that they'd added Thursdays to their schedule.

Again, I'm reminded of something else that makes Danes happy: belonging to groups that meet regularly, often weekly, throughout the year. When you belong to a group of people with common interests, you don't spend a whole lot of time planning to meet or searching for "your people." The plan is in place, and your people are there.

I think about the groups that have popped up around me and how much I look forward to being with them. From writing and reading to cooking and Pilates, being with people who share a common personal interest is refreshing. Rather than looking for cookie-cutter replicas of ourselves, we see one facet of a group that we can delve into with energy, as do the Monday Mountain Hiking Boys.

And one more thing the Danes regularly do: They get out in nature – no matter the weather. They say there is no bad weather in Denmark, just bad clothing. Bill says something similar about the weather in England; if you wait for a warm, sunny day to golf there, you'd go golfing only a few times a year. Layers and rain gear are key for golfing in England. You just need the right gear for the climate.

That morning, I walked alone on a snowy path. I got my heart rate up. I met a bunch of friendly strangers. I breathed in fresh air. I had sturdy boots and snow grippers. I felt like a Dane. Happy.

# Admiration

At 8:10 Monday and Wednesday mornings, the treadmill at the Y – in the second row from the window and the third one down from the end – is mine. Before I start walking, I grab a disinfectant wipe and give the treadmill a sponge bath. I watch others do the same after they work out, and I see their cleaning is not as thorough as mine. Some of them barely run the cloth over the handrests in front and on the side. They are the ones who barely come into physical contact with the machine.

That's not me. By the end of 45 minutes or 5K, whichever I can last through, I'm clambering onto the side rails of the treadmill. If I kick the speed up to do a 40-second "run" at 4.1 mph, I feel sweat pouring down. Certainly, some of it splashes onto the machine. I symmetrically wipe the sweat from my brow with the back of my hand. If I wipe one eyebrow and not the other, I have basically wiped one penciled eyebrow completely off my face.

Playing basketball in high school, I had a similar issue, only with baby blue eye shadow. I remember a girl who played forward pointing at me and laughing. I hadn't a clue why until after practice I saw one of my eyelids was baby blue and the other was not. Her baby blue eye shadow never smudged, for she never seemed to sweat. The complex has stayed with me, reminding me to either wipe above or below the brow. And in the event I think I've wiped one eyebrow pencil marking completely off, I try to do it evenly. I'm a bit overly compulsive when it comes to sweat and my eyebrows.

I play solitaire when I'm walking on the machine, so the same sweaty mitts that are wiping my brow move the cards on the treadmill's screen. With all this hands-on activity during my walk, I give the treadmill another good sponge bath when I'm done.

With 45 minutes of walking to nowhere, I do a bit of people watching as the usual crowd comes in. Same woman always reads. Same woman always walks. Same man always breathes in a heavy rhythm as he runs. Even if I can't see him, I know he's somewhere in the gym by his breathing. I note the defibrillators on the wall and am confident someone other than me has the know-how to use them should the need arise. The same two women run side by side and are able to talk nonstop.

Midway through my walk, two gentlemen come in and find neighboring treadmills. There is a generation between them. One must be in his eighties and the other in his late sixties. The elder of the two approaches his treadmill, hangs his cane on the side rail, and gets the machine in motion. No muscle-clad person in this entire place awes me as much as this gentleman. What do I want to be when I grow up? The 80-year-old who hangs my cane on the treadmill before I walk on that belt to nowhere.

I'm often rendered speechless when in the presence of amazing people. Twice in my life, I shook the hand of Captain James Lovell. In 1970, Captain Lovell was the commander of Apollo 13, a failed mission to the moon due to an explosion in flight. The ultimate mission of Apollo 13 became the safe return of the three astronauts on the damaged spacecraft. They succeeded by zipping around the dark side of the moon and using the moon's gravity to catapult them back to earth.

The first time I met him was just over a decade ago, and I didn't know he was going to be at the restaurant where we were celebrating a friend's 40th birthday. Captain Lovell's son owned the restaurant in a Chicago suburb. The second time, I called Captain Lovell's personal assistant to schedule a lunch with him so that my six-year-old space enthusiast Will could meet him. Both times I met Captain Lovell, I was like a starstruck teen. What does one say to someone who has flown around the dark side of the moon?

Simmering feelings of the same amazement strike me at the Y when this older gentleman prepares to board the treadmill next to me. I want to say something, but "Holy cow! You're amazing!" doesn't seem right. "You are my hero!" also seems a bit trite. Finally, one day we acknowledge each other with a nod, a smile, and a "good morning." The greeting didn't convey all the words that were bubbling in my head, but it didn't need to. I'll take the quiet strength of heart this man gives me as a kind of mentoring for my potential cane-bearing future.

Skiers can give me the same kind of goose bumps. In February 2018, we went out West with the boys for the first time to conquer big mountains in Utah. We skied all day, then watched the Olympics at night. The triumphs of snowboarders Shaun White and Chloe Kim, as well as alpine racer Lindsey Vonn, gave me energy and inspiration to take my sore body back to the slopes the next morning. Some stretches and a little ibuprofen were my prep each ski day.

The second day, Will and Liam took daylong ski lessons. Bill and I met them around 3:00 p.m. at the ski school base camp. With the lifts closing at 4:00, we watched many ski instructors returning with their students, from tiny three-year-olds with two-foot-long skis and no fear, to stiff adults who appeared to be trying to control the slick boards by curling their toes into their skis.

Then, seated skiers – paraplegic skiers, returning confidently and skiing alongside the crowds. They were led by paraplegic instructors as well as instructors on traditional skis. Some of these skiers were harnessed to the instructor who was skiing behind them, and some were on their own. No safety net. Comfortable in their ski gear, a seat on a ski, and a ski fit on the end of poles held in either hand.

In the distance, a group of four skiers with yellow signs on their fronts made their way down the hill. As they got closer, I could read the sign of the person skiing in the middle of the group: "Blind Skier." That skier was accompanied by an instructor and one person in front and one in the rear with matching signs: "Volunteer: Blind Skier." My gaze followed them as they skied past me in the same direction as the seated skiers. The back of the instructor's jacket read, "Park City – Ability Center."

These latter groups of skiers left me in quiet, tearful wonder. Whatever the catalyst had been for their disability, it was in the past. They had moved through the dark, burning moments of a life-changing event, or perhaps challenges that they were born with, to brave the ski slopes.

I lack words to wholly describe how the astounding courage and bravery of people – from the elderly man at the Y and Captain Lovell, to the paraplegic skiers and the solitary blind skier – affect me. Rather than continuing the pursuit for apt words, I simply acknowledge that their inspiring lives give me an abounding sense of peace, and for that I'm grateful.

# Skiing with a Beast

Looking for spring skiing with good snow, we landed at Killington Mountain in Vermont on a Sunday in February 2016. I had heard there was a thirty-foot base of snow. The forecast was for 39 degrees and sunshine. However, mountain weather changes faster than Midwestern weather. By midday, it was cold, snowy, icy, and cloudy. The top of the highest peak was never seen from the base lodge by the Malcolms' eyes that day. In fact, the slope was barely visible from the parking lot as Bill and Will started the day trudging toward the gondola line.

We split up as usual: three to the big mountain and one to the littlest mountain. In the gates to the quad chairlift for my second ride up the little mountain, I asked a mother–daughter combo if I could ride with them to the top. If an employee isn't telling people how to load, I believe from observation that the socially acceptable thing to do is to ask if you can join a group. As we three approached the front of the line, we left an open space between me and them.

Just as we started moving toward the loading zone where the chair would scoop us, a person zipped into that empty spot. I shifted slightly, making room as we loaded and settled into our flying chair. Pulling the safety bar down in front of us, I glanced to my left to make sure no one's poles were jammed in an uncomfortable position. I noticed our fourth joiner's coat. It was a tattered trench coat that came down to mid-shin. The seams were ragged. The material was canvas-like. My eyes moved up to the head. It was covered with a black helmet that was covered with gray duct tape. A gator, a half ski mask, covered the mouth and nose. I could see only eyes through the goggles.

The eyes stared straight forward. No words. Shifting my eyes to straight forward, I chewed on the visual. This looked like a homeless person on a ski lift. I didn't know if this was a male or female, young or old. All of us were silent on the quad, looking straight ahead. This could have been the quietest five minutes of my life. Or, as with every other ride up, I could start the small talk, for a chairlift is one of the few places I've found this to be a still-active hobby.

"Is this your first day at Killington?"

"Who, me??" replied a husky voice.

"Yes, you."

"Oh no, I've been skiing for two weeks! This is my last day. I pay $59 for a season pass. Can't beat it. This is the best mountain east of the Mississippi."

"Oh! Where are you from?" I asked the man. *And how is it that you pay only $59 when the average adult season pass is over $1,000?*

"Connecticut."

A little more ski talk moved to me asking, "Are you originally from Connecticut?"

"No, I was born in New York City" – *ah yes, I can hear that accent* – "then I moved to Pennsylvania before I moved to Connecticut."

"Oh, I was born in Iowa, and I live near Boston now."

"IOWA? I used to work in Iowa! I worked in Cedar . . . Cedar . . ."

"Cedar Rapids?!?!"

"Yes! I sold industrial machinery to the cornmills."

I chuckled, for I don't know much about Cedar Rapids other than the mills. Or rather the smell of Cedar Rapids because of the mills. The city eternally smells like earthy grains being slowly baked. It's the first Iowa smell that hits us after we land at the Cedar Rapids airport on our way to Mom and Dad's.

"Do you remember the smell of the mills?"

"Oh yes! They used to tell me if I was hungry, just to inhale!" Indeed, he knew Cedar Rapids!

As we continued with our small talk, I noticed a plastic card fluttering on the sleeve of his jacket. It was his season pass with his headshot. The petite gray head was that of an 80-year-old. But surely no . . . could he be? Above the photo were the words "BEAST PASS."

We wished each other well as we prepared to disembark. Did I notice the chair slow slightly as we approached the off-ramp? We both skied to the right after exiting the flying chairs. I stopped as usual to sort myself out before heading down the slope. I tried to adjust my poles and gloves quickly so I could watch this skiing enigma move down the mountain, but he disappeared over the hill on a blue slope of medium difficulty.

I scooted down an easy green hill, thinking by chance we might pair up again on the lift, but he was long gone by the time I made it to the bottom of our little mountain. On the way back up, I spotted him skiing down right under the chairlift. He looked like he had been born on those skis, as if he had sprung forth solidly from the mountain. With his long coat, he resembled a tree trunk traversing confidently, gracefully down the mountain.

With a little research, I discovered that there is only one way a person can pay only $59 for a Beast Pass to this mountain . . . as a Super Senior in the 80+ age group.

# Fierce Mountain Gnomes

In my first ski lesson with Bill more than twenty-five years ago, he taught me the importance of traversing. When the slope down the mountain looks too steep, look across the mountain and ski to the other side. I thought our night out snowshoeing from the top of Sterling Mountain at Smugglers' Notch in Vermont would include traversing leisurely down a mountain.

Around four on that crisp winter's evening, we grabbed snowshoes and boarded the chairlift heading to the top of the mountain. In addition to his snowshoes, Bill carried the small knapsack with our bottle of wine for dinner. Strong gusts of wind howled as we crawled, suspended high above the mountain, to its top. I kept thinking that the ride up is always the worst part of skiing, flying high above the slopes where there is no protection from the wind. I was sure this would be the most unpleasant part of the evening.

At the top, we exited the chairlift and met another couple who had been on this expedition several times. They led us to the warming hut where we would have dinner. We had a good laugh before our guides garnered our attention just before dusk to lay out the evening's itinerary. We would put our snowshoes on and leave them on for the rest of the night until we were at the bottom of the mountain. The women's facili-trees were out the door down a snowy path to the right. The men's were anywhere they felt comfortable. I am confident that none of us women fully cloaked in snowshoes ever used the trees.

Before dinner we were invited to go on a short scenic hike to get used to our snowshoes. Sounded like a grand idea. I was all for it.

Bill and I, together with our newly found friends from New York City, were probably the most mature people there. Consequently, we hung back and let those more youthful folks knock down the snowy path that hadn't been traveled for over a week. It was dark. The white snow was interrupted with black trees, and the contour of the path could be seen only by watching the human lump move in front of you.

The path went up and down, curved right and left. On the first hill up, we were like baby calves finding our new legs. I ventured too far to the left, and my leg disappeared into eighteen inches of snow.

Simultaneously, a guide in the back called out, "Just walk like a duck to get up the hill!"

Well, my duck legs were stuck, so I could only flap my wings. Which I did. Then my laugh muscles sucked all the power from every other muscle in my body. I soon sobered as I realized I had closed the path for fifteen people behind me. Tightening my core – thank goodness I'd gone to Pilates two days before – I heaved my leg up and back onto the path. Then came the downhill. Just as ridiculous. I skated between trees, following the guy in front of me, who was cussing. "Short and scenic" are not how many of us would have described this hike. We ended up on a frozen pond that was covered with deep snow. At that point, Bill and I knew the extreme benefits of lagging behind and letting the others tamp down the snow.

We trudged across the pond, trooped up a hill, and stopped momentarily to see the lights of Stowe over the top of the mountain. What was even more beautiful was the sight of the warming hut – until we opened the door. It was a sauna in there. I removed all the layers I could on the top. One more layer and I'd be down to my black bra. The snow pants weren't going anywhere as they were anchored on by snowshoes.

Dinner was delicious; however, we couldn't see anything but outlines and gray masses of what we were eating. The warming hut had no electricity. This was a true candlelit dinner. While I enjoyed the dinner, I realized how much I rely on my eyes to create the full gourmet effect of eating.

After dessert in the dark, we started our hike down. The first part was very steep, but I was confident that we would soon turn and it would get easier. Downhill was hard work, and I was overheating. I pulled my ski goggles off and gave them to Bill. Then my gloves. I kept waiting to traverse woodlands where the decline would even out. My knees screamed at me.

"OK, we are going to try to slide here!" called a guide. "Walkers to the left, sliders to the right!"

The idea was to turn turtle, hold your snowshoed feet up off the ground in tabletop position, and slide down the mountain. I watched thinking it might be a good alternative for my howling body parts, but no one could slide. There was too much snow on the slope. I took off my coat and tied it around my waist. Then my sweater. My hip joints were raw. I started to sidestep every few feet to relieve the pain.

I can't tell you how long it took to get down the mountain, whether it really was the 40-minute trip it had been billed to be. I knew my face was beet red. I kept thinking that thought I've had so many times flying when my sons were crying: "I will never see these people again." I did not take a picture of the aftermath. I needed no photo to remind me what this light-skinned, freckle-faced, 47-year-old woman looks like when overheated.

I wish I could say the landscape was beautiful. I'm sure it was.

I wish I could say that I can't wait to do that again. I'm sure I won't.

The morning after this adventure, I wrote in my journal:

"My thighs have been used as punching bags by fierce mountain gnomes."

# Swiss Chard with Cod

Last summer I orchestrated a symphony in my Dutch oven. Swiss chard with Cod. I first tasted it as a gift from a friend while I was going through chemo for breast cancer in 2009. Kate had prepared the base, so all I had to do was toss in the cod and Swiss chard, then boil it for ten minutes. I was a bit doubtful looking at the dubious mountain of Swiss chard, then a stranger in my vegetable vocabulary.

Three years after this meal, I picked up Swiss chard from my CSA, which stands for Community Supported Agriculture, where local eaters connect with the produce of local farmers. Having misplaced the paper recipe copy, I searched online for Kate's recipe: one with onion, fennel, tomatoes, chicken broth, and – the two stars – cod and Swiss chard.

Abundant power and confidence hit me while concocting this delicious dish independently. A friend made this for the bald me during that chemo era. Now, decked out with a full set of curls and cancer free, I'm making it for myself.

My Swiss chard from that Tuesday's CSA was a bit wilted when I got out my Dutch oven on Friday. Heck, what did that matter? It would wilt in the pot anyway.

My big wooden chopping board surfaced, and in seconds my kitchen started feeling the warmth of the prep smells. An onion finely sliced. A fennel bulb finely sliced. A few Yukon gold potatoes thickly sliced. It needed garlic to complete the chopping board warm-up. The rawness of aroma wasn't complete until the garlic was finely chopped.

Into the pot went a glug of olive oil, enough to wet the onions and fennel, speckled with salt and pepper. Those vegetables, nearly identical in looks but unrelated in taste, draw strings of memory. Until I met Bill, I hadn't cooked with onions. Until I sat around the table in an Italian woman's kitchen for a four-hour cooking class with Gail, a Wisconsinite who also loves to cook, I didn't know what fennel was, nor had I ever eaten so much olive oil in one sitting. At this, my first cooking class, Gail and I were sure that with our pores oozing oil, we'd easily slide out of the tight kitchen nook between bench and table.

The garlic, another ingredient Bill introduced to me, was hopping on the board, waiting to join the ten-minute sweat. It had to wait: that overanxious chopped bulb would burn and ruin the whole pot if introduced too early. It got thirty seconds to lightly dance, only after the onions and fennel finished their sweat and just before the tomatoes entered in the second movement.

Enter two pints of drained whole tomatoes that Mom had canned. If you aren't one of Mom's sons or daughters, sorry. You will have to make do with what you have. At this 2012 performance, the lid was marked "'09." Every time I open a pint of those tomatoes from Mom's garden, my fingernails curl under the seal and pry off the lids with a *pop*. Instantly, my left arm rises like a spring pulling the Ball jar to my nose. I close my eyes, and I inhale Mom's summer kitchen in Iowa. The second inhale is her winter kitchen, the smell of her chili prep. There is no sloshing these tomatoes from jar to pan. I smell until the memory is complete . . . until the strength of the aroma dissipates.

The tomatoes waltz with the onions and fennel, uncovered, for ten minutes. Great harmony rises in the steam. Popping bubbles make me think of a web of people: Kate, Gail, Bill, the Italian cooking teacher, Mom.

Then for the next layer. Lovely potatoes over the base of veggies, a twist of pepper and pinch of salt, enough chicken broth to cover, then lid on for a ten-minute simmer. My stock is made from a bouillon granule base, another trick of Bill's from twenty years ago.

And then, on the very top, those ingredients newest to my repertoire: fresh cod from the Atlantic and Swiss chard from my CSA. Local ocean, meet local farm. The cod waits patiently covered with a squeeze of lemon juice. Finally, the buzz of a ten-minute timer. Cod nestles on top of potatoes, and an enormous bunch of chopped chard fills the pot to the top. Lid on for ten more minutes.

Then the layers come out in reverse order. A plop of chard on each plate; a flaky, moist piece of cod next to the chard; then potatoes fished out of the sauce complete the trio.

The pan goes back to the burner still holding the sauce, with a lump of butter to add a little velvet. Then, uncovered, I boil it like hell for two minutes to take some of the liquid out and force the flavors into the ravished onions, fennel, and tomatoes. Finally, the burner is turned off, and a handful of chopped basil is scooped into the sauce. The ladling of it over the trio creates a crescendo to a dish too simply named "Swiss Chard and Cod."

This entertains every sense, lulling and teasing. Seeing the ingredients. Feeling the burn of the onion in the eye. Feeling the veg give way from whole to slices under deft movement of a big knife. Smelling the oils released with each slice and Mom's kitchen with each pop of a Ball lid. Hearing the sizzle in the pot with olive oil and then the simmering bubbles.

Taste. Yes, taste, but it's the last and nearly the least fulfilling. The other senses. Wow.

Heaped in a pasta bowl and served with multigrain bread and butter, this was "Swiss Chard with Cod." I had many guests joining me for that dinner. My husband, my mom, my Midwestern friend Gail, my New England friend Kate, the Italian cooking teacher, a Gloucester fisherman, and a local farmer. Some I know more intensely than others, but this smattering of people from the Midwest and the Northeast all had a hand in making this codfish dinner.

# Sand Dunes

In 2004, one of the reasons Bill and I considered New England's job market, 1,600 miles away from Midwestern friends and family, was the lure of the ocean. However, now, with the hum of everyday life, we might go months without physically seeing it or walking on the beach. A few years ago, I made a point of stopping at a beach once a month. In the off-season, it was easiest to stop at Revere Beach, which is only about fifteen minutes from our house. When I'm coming out of Boston on Route 1, small green signs with arrows point to Revere Beach, and if I turn right at the first sign, in a few blocks I see the Atlantic on the horizon. When I get to Revere Beach Boulevard, I hang a left and head north. If I stop and put my feet in the sand, I know from my beachcombing experience that here on an off-season day, I will find clamshells that are four to six inches wide.

On a true, planned go-to-the-beach day, preferably at low tide, my friend Kim and I load up the kids and head to *our* beach, forty-five minutes away. Wingaersheek Beach was the first beach we took our kids to. At low tide, the hard-packed sandy beach grows, seemingly pushing the water farther away. Simultaneously, a sandbar at least a half-mile long juts out into the shallows. To get a parking spot close to the beach, we leave town by around 8 a.m. in the morning. Unlike

Revere, Wingaersheek Beach isn't visible from the road or even the parking lot. Only when we waddling pack mules cross the boardwalk over the dunes does the sprawling horizon of beach and ocean come into view. Burdened with coolers, umbrellas, beach bags, shovels, and buckets, we hardly pause to see the ocean but continue trudging over the boards, then across the loose sand untouched by the tide, and finally to the hard-packed sand, where we stake out our little piece of real estate for the day.

We smear sunscreen on the kids before they run off. We drive umbrella poles into the ground and lay blankets out under those colorful round shades. We calculate the movement of the sun and where to place coolers so they will remain in the shade for a few hours. We set up chairs and anchor blankets with sandals and beach toys. Finally, we pull out beach towels and cover bags of crackers and chips such that the seagulls don't attack our compound. We know we'll see first-time beachgoers at some point in the day; we'll recognize them by the surge of seagulls viciously snacking on Goldfish crackers and potato chips under an umbrella whose owners are off wandering to the end of the sandbar.

With our spot set up, we are free. Behind us are the dunes, and to our right are rounded boulders taller than us. Thirteen years ago, we climbed these rocks while bent over holding our two-year-old's hands so they didn't slip off the edge. Now our kids disperse and conquer on their own. The wonderment of Wingaersheek is in its contours and in its shifting features created by the movement of the tide. Tucked into a large cove, the beach has thousands of minuscule tributaries of running water drawing symmetrical patterns in the sand as it scurries out with the tide. Dips in the beach and low spots by the boulders hold on to water and creatures, creating lively tidal pools. Their stillness contrasts with the nearby tiny streams of rushing water.

When I think of other beaches, such as Revere Beach, that are simple stretches of straight sandy shores met by rolling waves, the ratio of 50/50 comes to my mind – 50% land and 50% water. The strong draw of Wingaersheek is hard to articulate. When studying geography as a child, I remember maps of thin black lines showing the points where land meets water at the Pacific Ocean and the Atlantic Ocean. Similarly, I drew triangles to mark mountains. From my landlocked perspective, these geographical features were straight lines. But now I see continual mathematical morphing around me. At Wingaersheek Beach, the surface of land grows exponentially at low tide, and the length of walkable shoreline shrinks when the tide is high. On a given day, thousands of sand dollars cling to the sandbar. A week later, one small tidal pool is filled with a mom and a hundred baby sea stars that will disappear at high tide. On one October day, when I was at the beach by myself at low tide, I witnessed an outlier, one of those occurrences that falls outside the overall pattern of distribution: a deer swimming across the bay. I don't plan what to do when I go to the beach. I like the seeking and discovering, sprinkled with delightful surprise.

From the parking lot at Wingaersheek, there are a few boardwalk paths through the sand dunes to the beach. Through foot traffic and wind, the amount of sand on the boardwalk changes throughout the seasons. Access to the beach is limited to those boardwalks in order to protect the dunes; they in turn protect the interior land from flooding. On the dunes, short, dense, salt-resistant plants grow. Their roots help anchor the sand in place much the way prairie grasses once dug deep into Midwestern soil and protected it from eroding away.

Dunes along the coast are cordoned off. At Wingaersheek, wooden railings run along the edges of the boardwalks to the beach, and simple fences of small posts and a clothesline-like string run the length of the dunes along the parking lot side as well as the beach side. Some beaches have more structurally present fencing, meant to hold the sand in as much as to keep people out.

At the edge of a dune one day, at a beach that might or might not have been Wingaersheek, I abruptly stopped at a sandy intersection. I stood at the beach side of a dune where loose sand covered the beginning of the boardwalk and a vertical wood slat fence was half buried by a stubborn dune. The wood was gray and tired. Sand spilled through the slats onto the boardwalk, creating a small dune outside of its designated area. A single vine plant, about eighteen inches high, grew out of this pile of sand. The rounded leaves were dotted with small purple blossoms, their shape reminiscent of snapdragons. Set against the backdrop of gray fence and beige sand, the plant and flower were striking.

The vignette felt old and common, as if I had known it all my life. Yet, like the edge of a memory with my great-grandma Whittier, I couldn't snap into focus why I had this feeling of familiarity. I put words to the scene in front of me: a beach pea growing in a dune of fine sand that had usurped the weathered fence. Still, nothing. For years, I held the vision tight. Nothing.

My visit home to Iowa in February 2019 when my mom was ill unexpectedly loosened this still life, and it drifted into pieces: the fence, the dune, and the pea. My collective unconscious joined these with their cousins from a place some forty years away.

In the wintertime on the farm, a worn, wooden-slatted snow fence runs the length of the long gravel lane between the road and the barnyard, creating a border against snow blowing in from the wide-open cornfields. Feet of snowflakes accumulate like grains of sand in dunes and drift up the north side of the fence. Some snow fights through the slats, making small drifts that cling to the south side of the fence.

As for the beach pea, I'm reminded of a different season: an early summer morning in Iowa when pea pods hang from delicate, round-leafed vines in Mom's garden. A past scene unfolds.

I am sitting with Mom and her mom, Grandma Bauer, outside under a shade tree. The memory is quiet but for the rhythmic cracking open of pods and the pinging of sweet peas being shucked into metal bowls.

# A Menagerie of Recipes

Food has the power to hook a memory and reel it in to the present. Have you ever bitten into a piece of cake only to see a vision of your grandma standing at the kitchen counter hand-mixing a batter? Does a mouthful of buttered mashed potatoes bring to the table your grandpa shaking a hefty amount of black pepper over the white mass?

This menagerie of recipes has that effect on me. I make some of these dishes often, and there are some that I've never made – and probably never will. The latter remain too tightly sewn to another family member's kitchen.

In parentheses is the title of the essay that the recipe relates back to. I've either specifically mentioned these recipes in the essays, or they were inspired by what I wrote.

In some cases, it may be helpful to reread the essay before making the dish. Plus, definitely read through the entire recipe before making it: a useful lesson I learned in home economics class in high school. If you like photos with your recipes, full-color versions of these recipes are on my website, www.lindamalcolm.com, under the *Book* tab.

Here are a few other potentially helpful notes:
- Iowa's state bird is the goldfinch. Iowa's marketing slogan is "Iowa: Fields of Opportunity." Iowa's

state flower is the wild prairie rose. Iowa's state oven temperature is 350 degrees.

- In Iowa, a pan is a pan, whether used on top of the stove to make risotto or to bake a cake in the oven. As a friend from Iowa recently pointed out, *pot* is something people smoke. However, in recent years, I have incorporated *stockpot* into my kitchen vocabulary. And, of course, *Crock-Pots* are standard winter cooking vessels.

- I have yet to successfully soften butter in the microwave; I'm capable of only *melting* butter in that powerful box. Consequently, for recipes calling for softened/room temperature butter, I highly recommend leaving it out on the counter for a few hours or overnight.

# Lefse

("Preface" – p. ix)

Unlike the traditional making of lefse, I don't use a potato ricer, a lefse grill, or a lefse stick to flip the lefse. I have a potato masher, a cast-iron skillet, and a big hamburger-flipping spatula. My lefse is only as big as what will fit in my 10-inch skillet.

The ingredients are from the card in my circa 1982 brown sturdy plastic recipe box – with a couple adjustments: I go light on butter and don't add sugar to the dough since the final step before eating lefse is to top it with those two ingredients.

There's no name in "From the Kitchen of . . ." but I know this recipe is from a college friend's grandmother who was about 80 years old when I received the recipe in the late 1980s.

## Ingredients

2 pounds peeled potatoes
2 T. unsalted room temperature butter (at room temperature only because it melts into the potatoes quickly and easily)
¼ c. heavy cream
1 t. salt
1 ¾ c. flour
At least a cup of additional flour for rolling the lefse dough
Soft butter and sugar for serving

Boil the potatoes until mashable, then drain and return to the pan. Turn the heat off but keep pan on the hot burner while mashing the potatoes. The residual heat helps make the spuds fluffy while mashing them.

Stir in butter, cream, and salt. The potatoes will look dry and gummy. Transfer them into a big bowl to cool. Over the course of an hour or so, I make several cuts through them with a stiff spatula to let heat escape. Once completely cool, cut in 1¾ c. flour with the spatula. Use hands to knead in the last bits of flour and to form a ball of dough.

Preheat a cast-iron skillet on a medium-high burner before rolling out the first piece. Generously sprinkle flour on the counter, and pull off a large walnut-sized piece of dough. Roll it into a ball, flatten it into a patty, and flour both sizes before rolling. On the first or second roll, the dough will stick to the rolling pin; peel it off and reflour both sides of the dough. Roll it into a very thin circle, similar thickness to that of a flour tortilla.

Carefully move it from the rolling surface to the palm of your hand; then gently flip it from palm to palm to shake off excess flour.

Dry fry the lefse, checking it after about 30 seconds to see if it has browned. It will bubble a bit as it cooks. Flip and repeat on the second side.

Stay near the stove to watch the lefse, and reduce the heat to medium if it browns too quickly. We are really cooking flour here, so no flash browning – that won't give the lefse enough time to actually cook.

As the lefse cooks in the skillet, roll out the next one. This recipe makes around 20 pieces of lefse, so be prepared to stick near the stove for a good half hour. When burned flour accumulates in the pan after dry frying a few pieces of lefse, I carefully hold the pan over the sink and wipe the flour out with a dry paper towel.

When both sides of the lefse are covered with brown spots and it smells toasted, remove from the pan and place on a dinner plate. The hot pieces of lefse can be stacked on top of one another.

For the buttering and sugaring, put the lefse on a flat surface (the counter) to spread the butter edge to edge and sprinkle on the sugar. Fold the lefse in half, and then in half again. This pie-wedge shape keeps the butter from leaking out as it would if the lefse were rolled like a wrap.

For any lefse not eaten directly from the pan, cool, cover, and refrigerate. To eat later, pop a piece of lefse in the microwave for about 45 seconds to reheat.

We've tried cinnamon and sugar as well as jam on lefse, but I always revert to the way I first ate it . . . with butter and sugar.

# Irish Potato Chowder

———◆———

("Preface" – p. ix)

Over a decade ago, our family went from all adults – my parents, me and my three siblings, plus our spouses – to a lively family with seven grandkids.

For many years, we celebrated Christmas on Christmas Eve. All afternoon, Mom would be at the helm in the kitchen making a wonderful roasted turkey, beef, or ham dinner. We would eat, then wash dishes and pans and china and dessert bowls and more pans. Then, we would put to soak the scalloped corn pan and the roaster. When the grandkids came along, all of this washing took place while they hovered like hungry beasts – despite having just eaten – asking when we were going to open Christmas presents.

Now that there are seventeen of us, there are more holiday schedules to consider. Fortunately, Mom and Dad say they don't mind when we celebrate Christmas, just that they want us all together at some point. We approached the food the same way: We needed a meal, but did it need to be the traditional Christmas dinner?

We landed on the idea of a soup supper that involves far fewer pans to wash up after we eat. Now those traveling to Mom and Dad's that day contribute in a smorgasbord fashion, bringing shrimp cocktail, deviled eggs, homemade pies, and rolls for dipping in the soups.

Usually Mom, my sister, and I make the soups: chili, oyster stew, and potato chowder. I introduced Terese Allen's **Irish Potato Chowder** the first year of the soup supper. Since then, I have occasionally wondered if I should switch it out – if after a decade, perhaps people are tired of it. Yet every year before I even step foot on a plane at Logan bound for the Midwest, my brother and I have the same phone conversation. "Hey, Linda, about Christmas. . . . Are you doing that potato soup this year?" I hear the want in his voice. "Yup!"

I like to make a double batch of potato chowder the day before our Christmas celebration. Like many other soups, this one tastes even more delicious if the flavors are left to meld a day before serving it. When the chowder is done, I transfer it to a Crock-Pot to free up the pan for the next soup; then I stash the covered Crock-Pot in the van outside overnight – a benefit of winter in Iowa – so as not to take up fridge space. The next morning, about seven hours before we eat, I bring it in and let it set for an hour or so to get over the deep-freeze chill. Then I turn the Crock-Pot on high to reheat. Once it's heated through, I turn the temperature to low and let it hold there until we eat.

This layered creation has become one of the smells I now associate with Christmas. Some soup recipes are all-ingredients-in-the-pan, stir, and forget it. This dish comes together in sweet layers of time and patience, beginning with the mingling of vegetables and herbs in the deep well of the stockpot and followed by the release of a meandering bouquet up those steep metal walls.

I follow this recipe to the letter, for the creator, Terese Allen, has it refined to perfection. We keep the basil, parsley, chives, and ground white pepper in an **"Irish Potato Chowder"**–labeled baggie in Mom's pantry so they are at hand in December, making it easy to check inventory before cooking. Don't be afraid of the word *roux* or the hot pepper sauce. The roux is easy-peasy and beautifully golden brown when it comes off the heat. As for the hot pepper sauce, in this big of a batch of chowder, it does not make the chowder spicy; rather, it makes people think, *Hmm, there's something in here I can't quite put my finger on.* That little ingredient works the same as the last splash of cream in **Mushroom Risotto** and the final pat of butter in the sauce for **Swordfish with Tomatoes and Capers**.

Recipe for **Irish Potato Chowder** reprinted with permission from *The Ovens of Brittany Cookbook* by Terese Allen (Amherst Press, 1991).

*Excellent!*

14

# Irish Potato Chowder

### Serves 6

Dbl

7 tablespoons butter, divided
7 tablespoons flour
1 cup chopped onion
⅔ cup diced carrots
⅔ cup diced celery
1 teaspoon dried basil
1 teaspoon dried parsley
1 teaspoon freeze-dried chives
4 cups vegetable or chicken stock
5 cups peeled, diced potatoes (about 1¼ pounds)
3 cups milk
½ cup sour cream
⅛-¼ teaspoon hot pepper sauce
Salt and ground white pepper to taste

1. To make roux, melt 5½ tablespoons butter in a small sauce pan. Stir in flour until well blended. Cook over low heat, stirring often, for 3-5 minutes. Remove from heat and set aside.
2. Melt remaining 1½ tablespoons butter in a soup pot; add onions, carrots, celery, basil, parsley and chives; cook about 10 minutes.
3. Add stock and potatoes and simmer until potatoes are tender (about 15-20 minutes).
4. Stir in milk; return to simmer and whisk in roux until liquid is thickened and smooth. Simmer 10 minutes, stirring occasionally, then add sour cream, hot pepper sauce and season to taste with salt and ground white pepper.

*"Eats first, morals after."*
—Bertolt Brecht, *The Threepenny Opera*, 1928

233

# Braised Roast Beef

———◆◆◆———

("Meat and Potatoes" – p. 2)

I do not have a recipe for **Braised Roast Beef**, nor do I make it. It's one of those meals that I associate with seventeen people sitting in Mom and Dad's kitchen/ dining room. In this big open room, the oval oak kitchen table, with a wide claw-footed pedestal, can seat nine. Great-Grandma Whittier's oak dining room table slid up next to the kitchen table can seat eight.

The four legs on Great-Grandma's table have casters that no longer easily roll. However, this table has a beautiful gleaming dark oak shine; the wood was refinished about ten years ago by an Amish woodworker who lives near Mom and Dad. Usually it's a square table in the dining room against the far west wall under the windows, where it soaks up the late afternoon sun.

For family dinners, we gently lift and shuffle the table into place next to the oval table. From underneath Mom and Dad's bed, we slide out two leaves individually wrapped in blankets. We pull the tabletop apart, and, being careful to match pegs to holes, we insert the leaves. Then, with smooth pressure, we push together the sides of the table and make the cracks as small as possible. This slow and steady maneuver results in the creation of a rectangular table.

I know this much detail about the tables because I help set the table, but I do not braise the beef. Here's the recipe in the form of an email dialogue between Mom and me.

Me: Hi, Mom. A few people have suggested I include a recipe section in my book. Could you send me instructions on making your roast beef? And what breed are the beef cattle – Angus, right?

Mom: Oh! What a cool idea! Angus cattle. I use **garlic powder** and **pepper** on the beef. Also, **bay leaves** with it is good, too. I like to cook it the day before I am going to use it; that way it slices really well. You can cover it with gravy and reheat it 45 minutes to an hour. It is really tender with or without gravy, as long as it has some liquid.

Me: About the beef . . . What cut? How big? How much water do you put in? Do you cover it? How long do you cook it? 350?

Mom: I like the **arm roast, usually 3 lbs**. Thaw and bake at 350 degrees for three hours. Leave it open to brown, and then cover it about halfway through. It should reach temperature of 165. I would say about **3 cups of water**.

A couple notes . . .

Notice that Mom thaws the roast before baking it. If you, like Mom and Dad, raise your own beef and keep those beautiful white packages of various cuts in your ginormous deep freeze, you, too, would start by thawing the roast. For the rest of us, buy the roast at the store and continue on with the directions after "Thaw."

# Cranberry Scones

———◆———

("Cream" – p. 16)

Making clotted cream from scratch is not an adventure that's in my near future, especially since Devonshire clotted cream is readily available online and in specialty food stores.

As for scones, I tried this recipe years ago, and it was delicious. Made with cranberries, these scones have more flavor than the typically plain scones I've had with cream tea in England. This seems a fitting recipe to share since cranberries are a major crop in Massachusetts.

Regarding the buttermilk in this recipe, I never buy it. Since my elementary school friend gave me her recipe in school for *Salad Oil Coffee Cake* with the instruction to "make" buttermilk by adding 1 Tablespoon of white vinegar to a cup of milk, that's the only "buttermilk" I've ever used.

Recipe for **Cranberry Scones** is reprinted with permission from *Savor the Flavor of Oregon* by Junior League of Eugene (Oregon) (Koke Printing Company, 1990).

**Ingredients** (Yield: 1 dozen)
1 c. cranberries, fresh or frozen
3 c. flour

½ c. sugar

1 T. baking powder

¼ t. salt

½ t. baking soda

¾ c. butter or margarine, softened

½ c. chopped pecans or walnuts

1 ½ t. grated orange rind

1 c. buttermilk

**\*\***

1 T. milk

1 T. sugar

¼ t. cinnamon

⅛ t. nutmeg

In a large bowl, blend flour, sugar, baking powder, salt, and baking soda. Cut butter into flour mixture until it becomes a coarse crumb texture.

Stir in cranberries, nuts, and orange rind. Add buttermilk and mix with a fork until moistened. Gather dough into a ball and place on a floured board. Roll or pat into a circle ¾-inch thick. Cut into 12 pie shaped pieces.

Place on a greased baking sheet 1½ inches apart. Brush tops of scones with milk and sprinkle with sugar, cinnamon, and nutmeg mixture. Bake at 400 degrees for 12 to 15 minutes until lightly browned.

# Mushroom Risotto

———◆———

("Morels" – p. 30)

Rice, whether brown, jasmine, basmati, or Arborio, was not part of my diet growing up. Throughout the year, we ate primarily what we grew or raised. Mom didn't have a rice paddy, but she did have a garden filled with rows and rows of potatoes. When dug up, those hearty spuds would last for months spread out on the cool floor in the basement. It wasn't until well into my thirties that I discovered the soulful cooking of Arborio rice, named after the town where it was first grown near Milan, Italy.

Similarly, aside from morels in the spring, the only other mushrooms we had growing up were small cans of sliced, shrunken button mushrooms that Mom used on pizza. I had my first sautéed fresh button mushrooms when I was a student at Luther College in the mid-80s. While I do not recall the main dishes served in the on-campus restaurant, Peace Dining Room, those buttered mushrooms remain vivid. When I lived in Illinois, I slowly discovered other fresh mushrooms – shiitake, cremini, and portobello. Then when we moved to the East Coast, I found more exotic mushrooms in specialty grocery stores and public markets.

No matter the type of mushroom, simply slicing and frying them in butter, sprinkling them with a little salt and pepper, then serving them alongside a juicy steak is delicious. However, exotic mushrooms perform well in bigger productions, like **Mushroom Risotto**, which is a symphony of flavors.

My rule of thumb: With mushrooms that feel as sturdy as or sturdier than a button mushroom when I slice them, I sauté them, remove them from the pan, and add them back with the wine as the rice is starting to cook. For more delicate mushrooms, I sauté them briefly (separately from the sturdy ones) and add them back to the pan with the last ladle of broth that finishes off the risotto.

## Ingredients

3 c. chicken stock (see **Waste-Not-Want-Not Chicken Stock** recipe, p. 246 – or use canned)

Large pinch of saffron

Olive oil

Stick of butter (may or may not need all of it)

2 pounds of mushrooms, brushed off with a paper towel and sliced or pulled apart into small pieces

½ c. chopped onions

1 c. uncooked Arborio rice

¾ c. medium or dry white wine

⅛ c. half-and-half or cream

¾ c. Parmesan cheese

In a medium-sized pan, combine chicken stock and saffron, heat to a simmer, keeping the lid on so the stock doesn't evaporate. Saffron will dissolve in the chicken stock.

In a large pan over medium heat, add 3 T. of olive oil and 3 T. of butter; then sauté the mushrooms until they are shiny (refer to note above about sturdy vs. delicate mushrooms). Add more olive oil and butter if they seem too dry to cook down. When softened and slightly browned, transfer mushrooms to a bowl and set aside.

To the pan, still over medium heat, add 3 T. olive oil, 3 T. butter, and the chopped onions. Stir and cook until the onions sweat and start to become translucent. Do not brown. Add the sturdy mushrooms and the Arborio rice. Stir to coat the rice with the oil. When the rice sounds a bit like glass clicking on the side of the pan, add the wine. Stir frequently as the rice soaks up the wine.

When the wine has been absorbed, ladle in ½ c. of chicken stock and cook, stirring frequently until most of the liquid is absorbed. Adjust heat to keep the rice at a constant simmer; this may mean reducing heat to medium-low if it starts a rapid boil.

Add another ½ c. of chicken stock, again stirring frequently. Continue adding stock in this manner. When adding the last ½ c. of stock, gently add the more delicate mushrooms to the risotto.

Throughout this entire half-hour-ish process, keep a lid on the simmering chicken stock but no lid on the risotto.

When most of the moisture has been absorbed, the risotto will be creamy. Remove risotto from the heat and stir in the half-and-half/cream and the Parmesan cheese. To serve comfort style, dish up in soup bowls rather than on a plate, and eat with a spoon.

# Devil's Food Chocolate Cake

———◆———

("Black Dirt" – p. 38)

I remember Mom making devil's food chocolate cake for birthday celebrations as well as an any-day dessert. She used a recipe out of her standard household cookbook. I wasn't able to get permission to reprint that recipe, but after digging around in my stash, I discovered a "recipe" for Devils Food Cake in Grandma Mills's handwriting. It was just a list of ingredients, no directions.

Finding this card reminded me of how solitary life on the farm was for Grandma Mills when she was raising her family and farming with Grandpa. She and Grandpa did not go out to dinner with friends on Saturday nights, nor did they go to church on Sundays. She did not have a best friend or set of neighbors she regularly visited. The women's voices that I remember in Grandma's kitchen came from the AM radio show The Open Line. This program was on WMT, a Northeast Iowa radio station, and Grandma listened to women call in to talk about and read off their recipes. This was a one-sided social outlet for Grandma.

I can envision Grandma quickly jotting down this list of ingredients as they were broadcast by another farm woman.

*Devils Food cake*
½ c. cocoa
½ c. hot water
1 c. sugar
2 tbsp. lard or butter
2 eggs
1 c. sour cream or milk
1 tsp. soda.
2 c. flour
1 tsp. vanilla.

The instructions weren't important; they were known: Mix all ingredients together, pour into a greased 9" x 13" pan, bake at 350 degrees for approximately 30 minutes or until a toothpick comes out clean. Frost or serve unfrosted with vanilla ice cream.

In a large mixing bowl, I added one ingredient at a time and hand-whisked it into the batter. I upgraded the cocoa to Dutch process and the vanilla to Mexican, 35% alcohol; then I baked it for exactly 30 minutes.

As for the topping, I discovered that mint chocolate chip ice cream made by the Connelly brothers on their dairy farm in Temple, New Hampshire, works just as well as the vanilla ice cream did from the Schwan's man years ago.

# Mom's Buns (My Aunt's Dinner Rolls)

***

("Carbs! Glorious Carbs!" – p. 45)

I could have included a dozen recipes from that hot summer day when our family got together for a potluck in the park. However, I chose to share my biggest guilty pleasure: my aunt's freshly made dinner rolls, or as she calls them **Mom's Buns**, as the recipe was passed to her from her mom.

## Ingredients

¾ stick butter, divided
1 c. milk
4 ½ – 5 c. flour, divided
½ c. sugar
¾ t. salt
2 pkgs. rapid-rise yeast
1 c. hot water

Preheat oven to 375 degrees. Heavy-duty mixer such as KitchenAid is helpful.

Melt butter in milk in microwave. In a mixer bowl, combine 1 c. flour, sugar, salt, and dry yeast. With mixer on low, slowly add milk with butter and hot water. Allow to mix 3–4 minutes; scrape down bowl. Add another 1 c. flour. Mix for 3–4 minutes; scrape down bowl.

Slowly add additional flour ½ c. at a time. Allow dough to become smooth between additions. The dough should pull away from the sides of the bowl. Allow to mix until smooth. Total mix time is about 15 minutes.

Place dough in a large greased bowl; cover with a towel. Place bowl on rack over bowl of hot water to rise, 30–40 minutes. Punch down. Form into 24 rolls and place in a 9" x 13" greased baking pan.

Cover and allow to rise again for 30 minutes over bowl of hot water. Bake for 15–20 minutes or until tops are nicely brown. Melt remaining ¼ c. butter and brush over rolls.

# Waste-Not-Want-Not Chicken Stock

---

("A Fowl Story" – p. 54)

Never do I feel so connected to Great-Grandma Whittier, Grandma Bauer, and Grandma Mills as when I boil chicken bones in water. For it is then that I practice "waste-not-want-not" – more than any other time in my kitchen. The aroma of that bubbling pot echoes their kitchens and brings those farm women back into my life. The hands of cooking time slow to a lifetime ago.

I buy a **roasted chicken**, and my husband Bill, knowing my dislike of handling whole chickens, pulls it apart. He saves the meat in one container and plops the bones and skin into my deep stockpot that easily holds 11 cups of water. Then I take over. I dump all the **residual juices** from the chicken container into the stockpot; add 11 cups of **water**; add 1 quartered **onion** – skin and all; and add two unpeeled **carrots** and two **celery** stalks that I've broken in half by hand. Finally, if I have it on hand, I stir in 1 heaping teaspoon of **chicken stock base**, a paste found in the chicken stock aisle; it's a power boost for the chicken stock. I cover the pot and crank the heat up to bring it to a rolling boil; then I reduce it to a moderate simmer and leave it for 1 hour.

After the hour simmer, I turn off the heat and let the pot hang out for an hour or so on the stove. Then I put a large colander in my huge stainless steel bowl, carefully pour in the stock, and then dump the bones and vegetables into the colander. I carefully lift the colander up to drain all the stock; then I set it in the sink to cool. When cooled, I throw away the bones and vegetables, for their job is done.

From here, I either put the stock back in the pot to make **Chicken Soup** (p. 248), or I let it cool in the bowl, then pour it into quart containers to freeze for later.

# Chicken Soup (Rice or Noodle)

("A Fowl Story" – p. 54)

Everyone should have a go-to chicken soup recipe. I didn't realize that until the end of 2009 and the beginning of 2010 – when friends and neighbors delivered chicken soup to me each week that I had chemo. Throughout those eight rounds of chemo, I was amazed that every single person's soup was slightly different. Studying recipes and chatting with friends about how they make chicken soup, I've landed on this as my go-to recipe.

While it calls for "cooked" noodles, I often cook the noodles right in the soup. One of the best things about this recipe is that it freezes well at various stages: cooked only through veggies, or through chicken, or after adding rice. It doesn't freeze well with noodles; they wilt and disintegrate. Add lime juice after reheating it, not before freezing it.

A batch of **Waste-Not-Want-Not Chicken Broth** (p. 246) or 10 c. canned broth
1 ½ c. sliced carrots
¾ c. sliced celery
1 onion, chopped
1 bay leaf
¾ t. freshly ground black pepper

1 t. dried thyme leaves
Roasted chicken (skinned, pulled off bone, and broken up into bite-size pieces)
3 c. cooked rice OR 3 c. egg noodles, cooked al dente
2 T. lime juice from little green squeezy bottle
Salt to taste

In a big stockpot, add chicken broth, carrots, celery, onion, bay leaf, and black pepper. Pour thyme leaves in palm of your hand and crush with other palm in a twisting motion, letting crushed leaves fall into the pot. Bring to boil, then simmer for 15 minutes.

Add chicken and then rice or noodles, and salt to taste. (If I make it with rice, I start with a teaspoon of salt and season to taste from there. With noodles, I start with ½ teaspoon of salt.) Heat through. Take off heat and stir in lime juice.

# Grandma Bauer's Homemade Noodles

("A Fowl Story" – p. 54)

This is another recipe I've never made but decided to share. I have a weakness for thick homemade noodles. So, much like goose fat roasted potatoes in England, it's best that I not make noodles at home.

One of my great aunts made the best tuna and noodles. I used to rave about her thick homemade noodles. Some thirty years later, she pulled me aside at a family gathering and – with a smile that never left her face – quietly confessed, "You know, Linda, I don't make those noodles. They're frozen!" I was shocked. Still, I'm guessing when she was younger, she, too, probably made noodles from scratch.

This recipe has been transcribed and passed along to us grandkids by my aunt, my grandma's youngest daughter.

Makes 6–7 cups of cooked noodles. Recipe doubles easily; noodles freeze well, cooked or uncooked. Allow 4–5 hours total preparation time as they have to dry. If using egg yolks, more water may be needed.

## Ingredients
Slightly more than 1 c. flour, plus more for rolling out
¼ t. salt
2 eggs or 4 egg yolks
Scant 1 T. water

Whisk eggs or egg yolks and salt until slightly frothy. Stir in flour until blended well. Next stir in water, which will make dough sticky. Then stir in a little more flour until dough is drier and forms in a good ball.

Divide dough into two balls. Roll each ball into about a 9" x 15" oval, making sure to roll it about as thin as cereal box cardboard. You'll need to add quite a bit of flour under it as you roll it out thin and flip it over several times. If it sticks, use a knife to loosen it.

When you have it thin enough, take one thickness of clean newspaper (not newsprint but rather the Sunday newspaper) and drape it over the back of a straight-backed kitchen chair. Then pick up the dough oval with the rolling pin and drape it over the newspaper.

Let dry in room air, 1–1½ hours until surface of dough feels dry. Flip oval over so the other side can dry for 40–50 minutes more. Dry until dough just starts to get stiff and holds its shape when picked up.

Transfer dough to cutting board and, starting with narrow end of oval, roll dough up tightly in jelly roll fashion. Slice roll into ⅛-inch strips. Grandma always said, "The thinner the noodle the better." (An aside: I beg to differ – the thicker the better for me!)

Uncoil each noodle strip and spread out on a cookie sheet or kitchen table to air dry for another 1–2 hours until noodles feel pretty dry to the touch. Cook immediately or freeze for up to 3–4 months in bags or airtight containers. This batch makes about a 1-quart freezer bag of noodles.

To cook noodles with chicken: Bring 3½ c. lower-salt chicken broth and pieces of cooked chicken to a boil. Then add half a batch of noodles; the other half may be frozen for later use. Return to a boil, cover, and lower heat.

Gently boil 25–30 minutes until noodles are tender and most of the broth is absorbed, stirring occasionally.

These noodles are also good cooked in beef and beef broth. In addition, they can be added to other soups and stews.

# Corn on the Cob

("Corn's On!" – p. 75)

Over many years, and through Iowa and Illinois and finally to Massachusetts, I've moved from boiling vegetables to more often roasting, sautéing, or steaming them. It's taken a while to find the sweet spot for cooking corn on the cob, but I've finally found it. I consider this a bit of a cross between boiling and steaming.

Husk **corn** and place it in a pan big enough so that the ears can be mostly covered by **water**. Cover and bring the water to a boil, then turn off the heat and leave the pan covered on the burner for 10 minutes.

With tongs, remove ears from water to a plate. To butter hot corn on the cob, put a big pat of softened **butter** on a piece of **bread** and roll the ear of corn back and forth in the bread.

# Baked Cod

("Midwest Girl Goes Shopping for Codfish" — p. 115)

When I buy a lump of fresh fish, I like to cook it immediately. No overnight reservation in the Malcolm fridge. June, Bill's mum, also loved fish, and she preferred to taste the fish over any other ingredient in a fish dish. I think of her when I bake cod or similar flaky whitefish. This is a light version of baked cod — no butter.

A sprinkle of **lemon pepper** over a pound of **skinless cod fillets** on my seasoned round metal pizza pan. (Put a light coat of **cooking spray** on unseasoned pans.) Bake at 375 degrees for about 15 minutes or until the fish flakes with a fork. Top with a squeeze of **lemon** when it comes out of the oven . . . lovely, as June used to say.

# Swordfish with Tomatoes and Capers

("Swordfish with Tomatoes and Capers" – p. 151)

Be not afraid of the fennel bulb. Until this recipe, I had rarely used fennel, but now we are friends. Chop the fronds off the top; then treat it much like an onion. I wash the bulb and do not trim any outer layers away. Cut the bulb into quarters, top down as the fennel bulb sits upright on its haunches, and then trim the core out, much like you trim the core out of an onion.

Smell the anise? When the onions and fennel go into the pan, stand by to stir, yes, but smell . . . smell . . . smell the changes through those ten minutes before the garlic is added. The onions and fennel morph into a mellowed-out version of their intense individual raw aromas. Then, with a little help from the oil, they sweat and start looking like one another – as if the oil emulsifies them into one visually indistinct vegetable . . . the fennion or the oniel?

Maintain this inhaling of ingredients with every addition from tomatoes to chicken stock and wine, and finally, basil and butter. Experiencing the stratospheres of aroma in this sauce is a cook's joy. Honestly, it just may be for this selfish reason that I make **Swordfish with Tomatoes and Capers** for guests.

I've considered making two batches of this sauce at the same time – one for that day's dinner and another to freeze for a future easy dinner. To freeze a batch, I would stop cooking the sauce after adding the tomatoes and cooking them for 15 minutes. Then, when I thawed it out and reheated it, I would proceed with the last two layers: chicken stock and wine, followed by butter and basil.

We have only a gas grill, not a charcoal grill as Ina refers to in her recipe. I grill 1-inch thick fillets on medium-high heat, 5 minutes per side. The fillets will continue to cook a bit when they come off the grill, particularly if you tent foil over them. Be careful not to overcook as overly done swordfish loses its flavorful juices.

(Reprinted from *The Barefoot Contessa Cookbook.*
Copyright ©1999 by Ina Garten. Published by
Clarkson Potter, an imprint of Random House, LLC.)

### Swordfish with Tomatoes and Capers

Serves 4

1 cup chopped yellow onion (1 onion)

1 cup chopped fennel (1 bulb)

3 tablespoons good olive oil

1 teaspoon minced garlic

28 ounces canned plum tomatoes, drained

1 teaspoon kosher salt

¾ teaspoon freshly ground black pepper

2 tablespoons chicken stock

2 tablespoons good dry white wine

½ cup chopped fresh basil leaves

2 tablespoons capers, drained

1 tablespoon unsalted butter

4 1-inch-thick swordfish fillets (about 2 ½ pounds)

Fresh basil leaves

For the sauce, cook the onions and fennel in the oil
in a large sauté pan on medium-low heat for 10 minutes,
until the vegetables are soft. Add the garlic and cook for
30 seconds. Add the drained tomatoes, smashing them
in the pan with a fork, plus the salt and pepper. Simmer
on low heat for 15 minutes. Add the chicken stock and
white wine and simmer for 10 more minutes to reduce
the liquid. Add the basil, capers, and butter and cook
for 1 minute more.

Prepare a grill with hot coals. Brush the swordfish with olive oil, and sprinkle with salt and pepper. Grill on high heat for 5 minutes on each side until the center is no longer raw. Do not overcook. Place the sauce on the bottom of a plate, arrange the swordfish on top, and garnish with basil leaves. Serve hot or at room temperature.

*Notes from Ina:*

*This sauce is also delicious with other grilled fish, such as cod or red snapper.*

*When it is too cold to grill outdoors, I use a cast-iron stove-top grill.*

# Grandma Bauer's Pie Crust and Apple Pie

<img — omitted>

("Scrabble Grandma" – p. 161)

This recipe has been passed along to us grandkids by my aunt, Mom's sister, who still makes pies using Grandma Bauer's recipes. Homemade pies are our holiday treat – whether Easter, Christmas, or any other time we come together for dinner. These are my aunt's written directions for **Grandma's Pie Crust and Apple Pie.**

## Ingredients
(Makes 2 crusts, aluminum foil pan size)
¼ c. shortening
2 T. butter
¼ c. water (just mix in enough to hold together)
1 c. flour
¼ t. salt

Cut shortening and butter into flour and salt until dough feels greasy and has lumps the size of small peas in it. Cut in more shortening if needed; better a little rich as you can add more flour when rolling. (The trick is you can mix the flour and shortening as much as you want, but you don't want to do much mixing after adding the water.) Slowly add the water, mixing with your hand just until dough holds together and you can form all of the crumbs into one smooth ball.

I prefer to roll out crust immediately; dough may be refrigerated 1 week or frozen 1 month. For 2-crust pie, break dough into equal halves.

Put dough on table on about 3 T. flour, spread out. Smash dough down with palm of hand, flip over, and press down again, trying to form dough into a circle. Now lift up piece of dough and spread flour underneath, maybe adding a little more, to the size of the pie plate. Roll with rolling pin that has been dusted with flour. Start in the middle and work evenly, trying to form dough into a circle. Flip dough once while rolling and put more flour underneath as needed to prevent sticking. Roll to size of about 2" beyond diameter of top of pie plate, and crust should be less than ¼" thick.

Lay rolling pin 2" from edge of circle; using table knife, loosen edge of crust, pulling it up over rolling pin, and then roll crust fully onto rolling pin. Center crust so edge is 1" past edge of pie plate and roll off into plate. Can lift crust gently to center it after it is down. Before adding filling to plate, roll out top crust to size 1" bigger than pie plate. Continue with the following **Apple Pie** recipe.

## Apple Pie

6-8 medium, firm apples (I prefer Jonathan, Granny Smith or Jonagold; you can use any apple that isn't too mushy)

1 cup sugar
1 tsp cinnamon
¼ tsp nutmeg
3 TB flour

Mix dry ingredients together; set aside. Core/peel apples, slicing into ½" thick slices. Spread 2 TB flour onto bottom unbaked pie crust. Fill 2/3 full with apple slices. Sprinkle half of sugar mixture over apples. Add remaining apples, heaping them over the top of the pie plate 1-2". (For apple pie you may need to split the 2 crust halves more evenly so the top crust will cover the heaped apples, and probably roll it 2" beyond the pan.) Sprinkle remaining sugar over apples, taking care not to spill it on edges of pie crust. Put on top crust, seal and crimp edges. Cut four ½" slices around crust to allow juice to run out. Sprinkle cinnamon and sugar over top. Bake pie on cookie sheet to catch drips in a 400 degree oven for 10-12 minutes to set crust. Lower heat to 350, cover edges of crust with aluminum foil to prevent overbrowning. Bake 50-60 minutes until fork inserted in steam slits reveals apples are tender and juice is coming out. Bakes best on bottom rack. Remove and let cool. Serve warm or cool with vanilla or cinnamon ice cream or cheddar cheese.

# Christmas Sugar Cookies

("A 25-Year-Old Piece of Oak" – p. 178)

A day baking Christmas cookies must include a frosted cutout sugar cookie. My sister-in-law shared these recipes for cookies and frosting with me many years ago; now they are the only recipes I use for sugar cookies. I think the almond extract gives the cookie a bit more interesting taste than traditional cookies made with vanilla flavoring. The almond in the cookie and the vanilla in the frosting complement each other really well . . . really, really well.

## Christmas Cookies

### Ingredients

1 c. sugar
1 c. margarine
2 eggs
3 T. milk
3 c. flour
1 t. baking soda
2 t. cream of tartar
1 t. almond flavoring

Combine flour, baking soda, and cream of tartar in a large mixing bowl. In a separate bowl, mix sugar, margarine, eggs, milk, and flavorings. Add to flour mixture. Combine and form a ball, cover, and let stand in fridge overnight. Roll out and bake at 375 degrees for 7 minutes.

## Christmas Cookie Frosting

### Ingredients

¼ c. butter at room temperature

2 c. powdered sugar

1 t. vanilla

2 T. evaporated milk

Cream butter and sugar. Stir in vanilla. Add milk gradually until frosting is right consistency. I at least double this frosting batch for one batch of cookies, but it is easier to mix one frosting batch at a time, then put together if you want.

# Kolaches

———◆———

("Skiing with a Beast" – p. 208)

The combined efforts of Mom and her two sisters resulted in a beautifully orchestrated cookbook of Grandma Bauer's recipes. Grandma's quilts were used as backgrounds for the recipes. What resulted is a treasure: a vivid tribute to Grandma Bauer's life through photos of family, quilts, and her recipes.

Granddad Bauer worked in Cedar Rapids, Iowa, where there was a large Czech population. Grandma often made these kolaches, which are a traditional Czech dessert. I have a feeling kolaches came into Grandma's repertoire via some connection with the Czech community. This is a perfect recipe for people who do not like overly sweet desserts.

Recipe **Kolaches from Mom** Serves____
INGREDIENTS

½ C warm water      3 C flour

2 yeast (small envelopes)   + 2 C flour
       dry yeast      ½ C wesson

1 tsp sugar   + ⅓C sugar    Oil

1 egg

1½ C scalded milk

1 tsp salt       Yields:
              5 doz

Mix warm water, yeast, & 1 tsp sugar, set off to warm. Scald milk and add salt and ⅓ C sugar and cool. Combine the 2 mixtures after the one cools. Stir in 1 egg, 3 C flour, ½ C wesson oil and additional 2 C flour to make a soft dough. After dough is mixed well, grease and let rise until double in bulk. Make balls walnut-sized

Recipe of dough and put on
INGREDIENTS greased cookie sheet and let rise, then push centers of balls down and fill with filling of your choice. (Cherry pie filling, thickened pineapple, apricots, prunes) Let rise again, then bake at 400° 350° until brown. Grease tops of kolaches with stick of butter or margarine after taking from oven. Put on rack to cool.

# Swiss Chard with Cod

———◆———

("Swiss Chard with Cod" – p. 216)

The essay of the same name sums up what this panful of joy means to me. I was unable to get permission to reprint the recipe; however, you can use the following link to find it. It's definitely worth the hassle of retyping – or you can go to my website, www.lindamalcolm.com, and click to this link from the *Book* tab.

http://archive.boston.com/bostonglobe/magazine/articles/2008/02/17/cod_with_swiss_chard_and_potatoes/

# Peas with Mint

("Sand Dunes" – p. 220)

Much like Bill's mom June loved to taste fish without a lot of interrupting ingredients, I like to treat peas the same way: simply. When I met Bill and we started cooking together, we often boiled frozen peas as an easy accompaniment to meals that we cooked together.

While boiled **peas** are tasty on their own, Bill's English method of adding **a sprinkling of dried mint** to the pan as they boil gives them a gentle nudge of additional flavor.

\*\*\*

*And finally, one last line of direction from Mom – and Grandma Bauer – suitable for any recipe you ever make . . . "Cook with love!" Then, whatever you are making, even if it burns a bit around the edges, will turn out alright.*

# Acknowledgements

This is the hardest section to right as "thank you" seems not to convey all that these individuals have meant to me in creating this book.

Without the tenement of place, these essays wouldn't be, and so tied to those places are the members of my family in Boston, Iowa, and England. My hope is that these writings honor my grandparents, great aunts, great uncles, and other special souls whose presence throughout my childhood grounded me. Thanks to all of my family – especially Mom, Dad, Bill, Will, and Liam – as well as friends who are like family, for adventures, traditions, and memories.

Without the courage to pick up a pen, these essays wouldn't be, and over the last decade, Jennifer Doudous has been my life coach and my confidant. Despite living in Paris, she has an ever-optimistic presence in my writing.

Without other writers, these essays wouldn't be, and I have been incredibly lucky to have landed among many talented people from my first writer's critique group – Mary Baures, Jenny Pivor, Loren Schechter, and Diane Sharpe – to those who have read and critiqued my writing as *Cornfields to Codfish* came together – Dom Caposella, Sally M. Chetwynd, Colleen Getty, Robert Harvey, Marc Olivere, Lisa Perron, and Stephanie Sears. Writing itself is a solo exercise; the ability to meet others with the same passion has been an immeasurable benefit – through their critiquing and, even more so, through their camaraderie. Special thanks to my college friend and fellow Iowan cook, Donna Boots, who critiqued the recipe section with me by phone.

Without their grace in allowing me to reprint recipes from cookbooks and recipe cards, the recipe section wouldn't be. With special thanks to Therese Allen, Ina Garten, the Junior League of Eugene (Oregon), and to family and friends who've shared their recipes.

Without the wrestling of essays individually and as a whole, this book wouldn't be. At the New York State Summer Writers Institute in 2018, Lorrie Goldensohn, author and associate professor emeritus of English, Vassar College, tutored me and gave me invaluable guidance in how to step back and evaluate the structure of this work.

Without my volunteer beta readers, the people who agreed to read my *Cornfields to Codfish* manuscript cover to cover, this book wouldn't be. Ever so much thanks to those colleagues and friends who slogged through with pen in hand: Sally M. Chetwynd, Colleen Getty, Marc Olivere, Loren Schechter, Jacque Stouffer, and Lily Yamamoto.

Without creative talent, those energized souls who've made my book cover and my website shine, this book wouldn't be. With humble gratitude for the creative gifts you shared with me: Angie Carlyle, cover photographer; Sally M. Chetwynd, cover designer;

Scott Levy, web designer; Helene Norton-Russell, author photographer.

Without thorough proofreading and a final read-through, this polished work wouldn't be. Thank you to ProofreadingPal, a web-based company in Iowa, for thorough line-by-line attention. Much thanks to my friend and fellow Iowan, Judy Eide Knowler, for her gracious eye in reading the proof one last time before it went to print.

Without the guidance of iUniverse, this book wouldn't be. Senior Book Consultant, Brad Wilhelm, and Offset Print Project Manager, Kara Nelson, swept in at the last hour to help get this book to market at a fair price and within a very tight deadline.

Without the support of my dedicated readers over the last decade, my writing, these essays, and this book wouldn't be. To you I say, no matter how many stories I tell today to convey my thankfulness, there will always be a vast space that I cannot fill, as much as I try to shovel in the words – it's an unending crevice. Always indebted to your kindness and friendship.

# Essay References and Sources

**Preface**

*Lutefisk*, (https://en.wikipedia.org/wiki/Lutefisk, May 23, 2019).

*What's Cooking America*, Lutefisk History and Recipe (https://whatscookingamerica.net/History/LutefiskHistory.htm, May 23, 2019).

**Meat and Potatoes**

*All-Geo*, The Driftless Area: Fewer Glaciers but More Topography Than the Rest of Minnesota (http://all-geo.org/highlyallochthonous/2010/11/the-driftless-area-fewer-glaciers-but-more-topography-than-the-rest-of-minnesota/, May 23, 2019).

*Untamed Science*, Decoding the Driftless Area (https://www.untamedscience.com/blog/decoding-the-driftless/, May 23, 2019).

*U.S. Fish & Wildlife Service*, Conservation Biology in the Midwest Driftless Area (https://www.fws.gov/fieldnotes/regmap.cfm?arskey=31497, May 23, 2019).

**Dancing with a Foreign City Slicker**

*Stevenage Borough Council*, Stevenage New Town (http://www.stevenage.gov.uk/about-stevenage/museum/47012/46962/47008/, May 23, 2019).

### Walking Beans

*Dave's Garden*, Corn Detasseling: Understanding the Basics (https://davesgarden.com/guides/articles/view/4341, May 23, 2019).

*Iowa City Press-Citizen*, Iowa Farmers Bringing Back Walking Beans? (https://www.press-citizen.com/story/news/local/2014/07/16/iowa-farmers-bringing-back-walking-beans/12764661/, May 23, 2019).

### *Cream*

*Visit Dartmoor*, Delicious Dartmoor map (https://www.visitdartmoor.co.uk/food-and-drink/taste-of-dartmoor, May 23, 2019).

*Visit Dartmoor*, Welcome to Dartmoor – The Heart of Devon (https://www.visitdartmoor.co.uk/, May 23, 2019).

Arthur Conan Doyle, *The Hound of the Baskervilles*, ed. Christopher Frayling (London: Penguin Books, 2003).

Philip Weller, *The Hound of the Baskervilles: Hunting the Dartmoor Legend: Being the Original Text of the Classic Story* (Devon Books, 2001).

*Michigan State University – MCU Extension*, History of dairy cow breeds: Jersey (https://www.canr.msu.edu/news/history_of_dairy_cow_breeds_jersey, May 23, 2019).

*Billings Farm & Museum*, Visit Billings Farm & Museum (https://billingsfarm.org/visit/, May 23, 2019).

**Field of English Flowers**
*wiseGEEK*, What Is Canola Oil? (http://www.wisegeek. com/what-is-canola-oil.htm, May 23, 2019).

*MayoClinic*, I've Read That Canola Oil Contains Toxins. Is That True? (http://www.mayoclinic.com/ health/canola-oil/AN01281, May 23, 2019).

*StevenageBoroughCouncil*. Stevenage New Town (http://www.stevenage.gov.uk/about-stevenage/ museum/47012/46962/47008/, May 23, 2019).

**At the Edge of a Memory**
*Iowa Public Television*, A Magazine Called *Wallaces' Farmer* (http://www.iptv.org/iowapathways/mypath/ magazine-called-wallaces%E2%80%99-farmer, May 23, 2019).

*Feedstuffs*, History of *Wallaces Farmer* (https://www. feedstuffs.com/wallaces-farmer-history, May 23, 2019).

**Wandering through Pastures**
*The Pennsylvania State University – PCU Extension,* Milk Components: Understanding Milk Fat and Protein Variation in Your Dairy Herd (https://extension.psu. edu/milk-components-understanding-milk-fat-and-protein-variation-in-your-dairy-herd, May 23, 2019).

*Health and Safety Executive*, Cattle and Public Access in England and Wales: Advice for Farmers, Landowners and Other Livestock Keepers (http://www.hse.gov.uk/pubns/ais17ew.pdf, May 23, 2019).

**Iowa Storms**
*Storm Prediction Center – NOAA/National Weather Service*, About Derechos (https://www.spc.noaa.gov/misc/AbtDerechos/derechofacts.htm, May 23, 2019).

**Slugs and Worms**
*The Old Farmer's Almanac*, Tomato Hornworms: How to Identify and Get Rid of Tomato Horn Worms (https://www.almanac.com/pest/tomato-hornworms, May 23, 2019).

**Jingle Shells**
*Cape Cod Times*, Slipper Shells Growth in Buzzard Bay Puzzles Researchers (https://www.capecodtimes.com/article/20151108/NEWS/151109497, May 23, 2019).

*ThoughtCo*, All About the Jingle Shell (https://www.thoughtco.com/jingle-shell-profile-2291802, May 23, 2019).

**The Whale Tooth in the Trunk**
*ThoughtCo*, Marine Life Glossary: Baleen (https://www.thoughtco.com/baleen-definition-2291694, May 23, 2019).

*Marine Dimensions*, What Is a Mermaid's Purse? (https://marinedimensions.ie/what-is-a-mermaid-purse/, May 23, 2019).

## Mother-in-Law's Tongue and Christmas Cactus

*Michigan State University – MCU Extension*, The Secret to Getting a Christmas Cactus to Bloom: Temperature and Light (https://www.canr.msu.edu/news/the_secret_to_getting_a_christmas_cactus_to_bloom_temperature_and_light, May 23, 2019).

## April Fresh Scent

*Merriam-Webster Dictionary*, Nosegay (https://www.merriam-webster.com/dictionary/nosegay, May 23, 2019).

## Swordfish with Tomatoes and Capers

*Food Network*, Swordfish with Tomatoes and Capers (https://www.foodnetwork.com/recipes/ina-garten/swordfish-with-tomatoes-and-capers-recipe-1945657, May 23, 2019).

## Lumps of Sugar

*The Cromwell Hotel* (https://cromwellstevenage.co.uk/, May 23, 2019).

*History*, Oliver Cromwell (https://www.history.com/topics/british-history/oliver-cromwell, May 23, 2019).

*The Comet*, Cromwell Hotel Reclaims Its Rightful Place in Stevenage Old Town's Heritage with Impressive Refurbishment (https://www.thecomet.net/news/cromwell-hotel-reclaims-its-rightful-place-in-stevenage-old-town-s-heritage-with-impressive-refurbishment-1-5236924, May 23, 2019).

## Getting to Iowa: Christmas 2015

*Merriam-Webster Dictionary*, Travail (https://www.merriam-webster.com/dictionary/travail, May 23, 2019).

## The Crash of the Christmas Tree

Margaret Rey and H. A. Rey, *The Complete Adventures of Curious George* (London: Carlton Books, 2005).

## Hiking in the Berkshires

Helen Russell, *The Year of Living Danishly: Uncovering the Secrets of the World's Happiest Country* (London: Icon Books, 2016).

## Admiration

*Smithsonian National Air and Space Museum*, Apollo 13 – AS-508 (https://airandspace.si.edu/explore-and-learn/topics/apollo/apollo-program/landing-missions/apollo13.cfm, May 23, 2019).

\*\*\*

With respect to privacy, names of individuals have been changed throughout these essays.